Europe, Discourse, Institutions

This book focuses on how discourse and various narratives contribute to the construction of the European Union as a political actor, thus seeking to challenge the more established approaches to the study of the Union. It sheds light on the way discourses about the European Union are created, perpetuated and then translated into policy outcomes. Most of the contributions attempt to account for the differences that usually arise between discourse and policy practices. The methods employed range from more traditional variants of discourse analysis to other more radical versions that emphasise power, or to critical or differential reading of policy narratives and ethnography. Policy areas such as trade, enlargement, foreign policy and the European Neighbourhood Policy (ENP) are discussed, while a particular interest is awarded to the European Parliament and the Commission. In doing so, the contributions shed light on the role discourse plays in relation to policies, institutional practices, and value representations at the European level. Moreover, the authors analyse the different actors and structures that create and perpetuate discourses within the EU, highlighting new insights that a focus on discourse can bring to the field of European Union studies.

This book was previously published as a special issue of *Perspectives on European Politics and Society*.

Cristian Nițoiu is Post-doctoral Research Fellow within the European Neighbourhood Policy Chair at the College of Europe, Natolin Campus.

Nikola Tomić has recently completed his PhD within the Department of Politics, History and International Relations at Loughborough University, UK.

Europe, Discourse, Institutions
Challenging the Mainstream in European Studies

Edited by
Cristian Niţoiu and Nikola Tomić

LONDON AND NEW YORK

First published 2015
by Routledge

2 Park Square, Milton Park, Abingdon, Oxfordshire OX14 4RN
711 Third Avenue, New York, NY 10017

Routledge is an imprint of the Taylor & Francis Group, an informa business

First issued in paperback 2018

Copyright © 2015 Taylor & Francis

All rights reserved. No part of this book may be reprinted or reproduced or utilised in any form or by any electronic, mechanical, or other means, now known or hereafter invented, including photocopying and recording, or in any information storage or retrieval system, without permission in writing from the publishers.

Notice:
Product or corporate names may be trademarks or registered trademarks, and are used only for identification and explanation without intent to infringe.

British Library Cataloguing in Publication Data
A catalogue record for this book is available from the British Library

ISBN13: 978-1-138-79316-3 (hbk)
ISBN13: 978-1-138-37934-3 (pbk)

Typeset in Times New Roman
by Taylor & Francis Books

Publisher's Note
The publisher accepts responsibility for any inconsistencies that may have arisen during the conversion of this book from journal articles to book chapters, namely the possible inclusion of journal terminology.

Disclaimer
Every effort has been made to contact copyright holders for their permission to reprint material in this book. The publishers would be grateful to hear from any copyright holder who is not here acknowledged and will undertake to rectify any errors or omissions in future editions of this book.

Contents

Citation Information	vii
1. Introduction *Cristian Niţoiu & Nikola Tomić*	1
2. Making the Mythical European: Elucidating the EU's Powerful Integration Instrument of Discursive Identity Construction *S. Anne Bostanci*	8
3. The Battle Against Unfair Trade in the EU Trade Policy: A Discourse Analysis of Trade Protection *Josué F. Mathieu & Sharon Weinblum*	21
4. 'Bursting the Brussels Bubble': Using Ethnography to Explore the European Parliament as a Transnational Political Field *Amy Busby*	39
5. Coordinative Discourses in Brussels: An Agency-oriented Model of EU Foreign Policy Analysis *Nikola Tomić*	59
6. The Narrative Construction of the European Union in External Relations *Cristian Niţoiu*	76
7. The EU and Russia: Competing Discourses, Practices and Interests in the Shared Neighbourhood *Vanda Amaro Dias*	92
Index	109

Citation Information

The chapters in this book were originally published in *Perspectives on European Politics and Society*, volume 14, issue 2 (June 2013). When citing this material, please use the original page numbering for each article, as follows:

Chapter 1
Introduction
Cristian Niţoiu & Nikola Tomić
Perspectives on European Politics and Society, volume 14, issue 2 (June 2013)
pp. 165-171

Chapter 2
Making the Mythical European: Elucidating the EU's Powerful Integration Instrument of Discursive Identity Construction
S. Anne Bostanci
Perspectives on European Politics and Society, volume 14, issue 2 (June 2013)
pp. 172-184

Chapter 3
The Battle Against Unfair Trade in the EU Trade Policy: A Discourse Analysis of Trade Protection
Josué F. Mathieu & Sharon Weinblum
Perspectives on European Politics and Society, volume 14, issue 2 (June 2013)
pp. 185-202

Chapter 4
'Bursting the Brussels Bubble': Using Ethnography to Explore the European Parliament as a Transnational Political Field
Amy Busby
Perspectives on European Politics and Society, volume 14, issue 2 (June 2013)
pp. 203-222

CITATION INFORMATION

Chapter 5
Coordinative Discourses in Brussels: An Agency-oriented Model of EU Foreign Policy Analysis
Nikola Tomić
Perspectives on European Politics and Society, volume 14, issue 2 (June 2013)
pp. 223-239

Chapter 6
The Narrative Construction of the European Union in External Relations
Cristian Nițoiu
Perspectives on European Politics and Society, volume 14, issue 2 (June 2013)
pp. 240-255

Chapter 7
The EU and Russia: Competing Discourses, Practices and Interests in the Shared Neighbourhood
Vanda Amaro Dias
Perspectives on European Politics and Society, volume 14, issue 2 (June 2013)
pp. 256-271

Please direct any queries you may have about the citations to clsuk.permissions@cengage.com

Introduction

CRISTIAN NIȚOIU & NIKOLA TOMIĆ
School of Politics, History and International Relations,
Loughborough University, UK

ABSTRACT   *This special issue surveys the ways in which a focus on discourse can bring new insights in a number of key areas in European Union studies. It claims that although increasingly prominent in recent years, discourse theory and discourse analysis are still at an infant stage in European Union studies. At the moment, three different research agendas and approaches to discourse theory in European Union studies can be identified: analysing discourses of national foreign policies and its relations with the European level, the discourse analysis of European identity and culture, and finally analysing discourse to explain governance and political struggle. This special issue focuses on how discourse and various narratives contribute to the construction of the European Union as a political actor, thus seeking to challenge the more established approaches to the study of the Union. It sheds light on the way discourses about the European Union are created, perpetuated and then translated into policy outcomes. Most papers attempt to account for the differences that usually arise between discourse and policy practices. The methods employed range from more traditional variants of discourse analysis to other more radical versions that emphasize power, or to critical or differential reading of policy narratives and ethnography. Policy areas such as trade, enlargement, foreign policy and the European Neighbourhood Policy (ENP) are discussed, while a particular interest is awarded to the European Parliament and the Commission. In doing so, the contributions shed light on the role discourse plays in relation to policies, institutional practices, and value representations at the European level. Moreover, the authors analyse the different actors and structures that create and perpetuate discourses within the EU, highlighting new insights that a focus on discourse can bring to the field of European Union studies.*

Although more and more prominent within recent years, discourse theory and discourse analysis are still at an infant stage in European Union studies. Similarly to social constructivism, discourse theory is not a general theory of European integration, but an approach useful in explaining or illuminating certain aspects of European integration and European Union politics. As spill-overs from IR theory, constructivism and discourse theory represent philosophical approaches which shed light on certain features of European integration (Risse, 2009, pp. 144–145). The social and political realities in general – and certain aspects of international politics and European integration in particular – are posited as constructs of groups or individual actors. The way through which actors in European Union politics create reality is through communication and practice. Discourse theory is thus relevant for analysing the discursive creation of meaning of the material world. Discourse as an important factor in analysing European integration has been pushed forward by authors such as Risse (2000), Diez (1999, 2001, 2005), Hay and Rosamond (2001), Rosamond (2007), Larsen (1997), Schmidt (2001) and Waever (2001). The aim of this special issue is to respond to the call of these (relatively few) authors to challenge the mainstream in European Union studies and to carry discourse theory and discourse analysis out of its infancy and into a mainstream approach to analysing the European Union.

At the moment, three different research agendas and approaches to discourse theory in European Union studies can be identified: analysing discourses of national foreign policies and its relations with the European level, the discourse analysis of European identity and culture, and finally analysing discourse to explain governance and political struggle (Waever, 2009). The first approach is most common, as it is closer to more traditional views on European politics – remnants of the dominant IR approach to European Union studies. It posits the national member states as unified actors in international relations (and European integration, as a subsystem of international relations). The research questions revolve around the mutual impact of discourses from the national levels and the European level. The literature on Europeanization is closest to this approach (Borzel & Risse, 2007; Goetz & Hix, 2000; Olsen, 2002; Featherstone & Radaelli, 2003; Radaelli & Schmidt, 2005). One of the main problems with this approach is that it sees discourses as a relatively stable variable in explaining developments in European foreign policy (Howorth, 2004). Besides using the term discourse rather loosely and sometimes even misplacing the term (replacing terms like rhetoric, identity or argumentation), it does not properly (if at all) pose the question how discourses are created and where they originate from, but rather take them for granted as the discourse of a member state in a given situation (Beland, 2009; Parsons, 2010). Such a broad definition of discourse, where 'it is "all discourse"' (Waever, 2009, p. 172), may make discourse analysis more approachable and available to scholars of European Union studies, but it takes away the potential depth of analysis. Another issue with this approach is that it focuses primarily on states as carriers of discourse, which similarly may be analytically more appealing, but this approach fails to take into account the more subtle mechanisms of discourse creation at the European level of policy making.

The second treatment of discourse in European Union studies poses questions of identities, of 'we' feelings and of the 'other' (Checkel & Katzenstein, 2009; Manners, 2002, 2006, 2010; Diez, 1999, 2001, 2005). Such an approach is relevant for providing the background information and ideational positions of actors in different policies of the EU. Actors create contexts and position themselves within them through discourse. The actors of the European policies create their own nature and role in the European polity. The third approach to discourse and European integration can be seen as a compromise between the first and the second approach, because it focuses on both discourses across national boundaries as well as individual national discourses, which can be seen as 'the discursive manifestation of multi-level governance' (Waever, 2009, p. 172) and political struggle across both the national and transnational (or supranational) levels of discursive action. Through this approach, discourses cross not just borders of states, but also different policy sectors. It postulates the existence of conflicting and discursively constructed 'polity ideas' which is a set of 'normative ideas about a legitimate political order' (Jachtenfuchs et al., 1998, p. 410). This treatment of discourse enables researchers to analyse European discourses both in depth and breadth. Such an approach helps explain both the interaction between the EU level and national levels of policy making as well as the construction of legitimizing ideas at all levels of discursive action.

More critical approaches, like post-structuralism have been commonly avoided in European Studies scholarship. The poststructuralist discourse theory of Laclau and Mouffe (2001) departs from the supposition that 'all social phenomena, objects and subjects obtain their meaning(s) through discourse, which is defined as "a structure in which meaning is constantly negotiated and constructed"' (Carpentier & De Cleen, 2007, p. 267). Discourse plays an important role in the construction of the identity of subjects/agents (in our case the EU) because identities are 'accepted, refused and negotiated in discursive processes'. Identity is thus not determined by economic or material factors, but in relation to other identities. While this categorization is useful to understand the different ways discourse can illuminate certain aspects of European Union politics, in practice one can witness the role of discourse cutting across these research foci (Schmidt, 2011). This special issue focuses on how discourse and various narratives contribute to the construction of the European Union as a political actor, thus seeking to challenge the more established approaches to the study of the Union. It sheds light on the way discourses about the European Union are created, perpetuated and then translated into policy outcomes, most papers trying to account for the differences that usually arise between discourse and policy practices. The methods employed range from more traditional variants of discourse analysis to other more radical versions that emphasize power, or to critical or differential reading of policy narratives and ethnography. Policy areas such as trade, enlargement, foreign policy and the European Neighbourhood Policy (ENP) are discussed, while a particular interest is awarded to the European Parliament and the Commission. In doing so, the contributions shed light on the role discourse plays in relation to policies, institutional practices, and value representations at the European level. Moreover, the authors analyse the different actors and structures that create and perpetuate discourses within the EU, in this way highlighting new insights that a focus on discourse can bring to the field of European Studies. The exploration of issues in each area of European Union studies represented in this special issue is seen as essential to the articulation of the interdisciplinary approach advocated here. The special issue seeks to transcend the common accidental character of interdisciplinarity centred on discourse in European studies (Rumford & Murray, 2003). Instead, we aim for a more programmatic scholarly endeavour, where discursive approaches are used in a conscious manner, which opens communication between scholars studying different policy areas of the European Union but are linked by a focus on discourse (Favell & Guiraudon, 2009).

The first article by S. Anne G. Bostanci contends that the mainstream theories of European integration are part of the same dominant paradigm. The article draws on Kuhn's work and demonstrates that the dominance of such theories as neo-functionalism and intergovernmentalism has eclipsed and marginalised other approaches and insights into the study of the European project. Hence, Bostanci proposes the development of new a paradigm which would open the way for currently neglected approaches to surface. The first steps in such an endeavour involves adopting a self-reflexive stance where the consequences of one's own views and approaches are foregrounded as the analysis unfolds.

More specifically, the article advocates a focus on the role of political myths which has the potential to shed light on the structural affective, as well as individual and collective identity-endowing dimensions of political discourse. However, this approach is plagued by a looming danger, namely the tendency to focus on the EU's discourses as part of the policy process rather than on their role as political myths – a tendency which is mainly informed by the dynamic and empirical character of the institutional realities of the EU. Bostanci further claims that myths are at the core of the EU's identity and ideology as they are constructed in relation to all policy areas and originate from a myriad of sources with the European Commission at the forefront. The article concludes with recognising the fact that a focus on political myths has started to permeate mainstream theories of European integration, but more rigorous and extensive theoretical and empirical research is still needed.

The following article by Josué F. Mathieu and Sharon Weinblum explores the way in which the European Union uses its Trade Defence Instruments as a way of fighting and limiting global unfair trade. Mathieu and Weinblum argue that precisely the target of these instruments – i.e., unfair trade – is at best an underspecified and confusing notion which has deep consequences on the way in which the EU designs its policies. Hence, the article proposes that an interpretive approach could bring to light new meanings that are linked to the concept of unfair trade. By combining the concept of 'floating signifier' with the concept of 'storyline' the analysis brings to light elements of the political and discursive reality of the European Union – elements which might have been overlooked by an endeavour meant to simply map the range of ideas which underpin a certain issue, such as 'unfair trade'. Empirically, the analysis focuses on the anti-dumping debates within the European Parliament, and finds that a certain interpretation of 'unfair trade' has become part of the mainstream and consequently reified by discursive and policy practice. MEPs have been reluctant to express and to articulate views dissenting from this dominant storyline which prescribes the rationales for trade remedies such as anti-dumping or countervailing duties. Mathieu and Weinblum envisage that the EP will not weaken the power and scope of the Trade Defence Instruments in the background of the modernisation process initiated by the European Commission. Moreover, the dominant understating of unfair trade and the subsequent trade remedies will at most undergo a limited and flimsy process of assessment and contestation.

The European Parliament is also the focus of the third contribution to this special issue, but presented from an inside perspective. Based on ethnographic research, Amy Busby provides a look into the daily activities and struggles of MEPs within the confines of the 'Brussels bubble'. Through the use of an ethnographic methodology fused with Bourdieu's framework for analysing social practice, the article engages in an insightful exploration of the everyday practice and political activities in the EU's most democratic transnational institution, the European Parliament. In her article, Busby first locates the analytical framework within the wider literature and describes its subsequent theoretical underpinnings. The ethnographic data presented in this contribution was gathered during a seven-month stay in Brussels where Busby served as an assistant for different MEPs, being immersed into the everyday practices and discourses of the European Parliament deep inside the 'Brussels bubble'. Within the article, ethnographic data is analysed by focusing on a number of concepts central to Bourdieu's framework in order to understand MEPs social practice and discourse: field, capital, strategies, habitus and doxa. Busby finds that the EP is widely viewed as the most democratic, egalitarian, cooperative and inclusive transnational institution within the EU.

Further, she notes that the most successful and effective MEPs in shaping the political agenda are those who have acquired political capital by either holding particular offices (such as the group leader or rapporteur) or have in time built a reputation as laborious, cooperative experts. This in turn reinforces the view that the European Parliament is a dynamic institutional and political setting where continuous cooperation and negotiation shape the everyday practice and discourse of MEPs.

The fourth article by Nikola Tomić also adopts an approach to analysing the day-to-day practices of agents. The focus of the article however is on less transparent institutions of the EU's foreign policy, in which ethnographic research poses greater difficulties, due to the sensitive and confidential nature of the policy process. Acknowledging the methodological difficulties, Tomić proposes an agency-oriented model of EU foreign policy analysis based on a constructivist ontology and interpretive methodology. The article discusses at first the contested concept of EU foreign policy and posits that the concept should be understood and defined along the lines of EU external action, which includes a number of policies from all three former pillars of the EU. With the concept of EU foreign policy delineated, the article continues on proposing an alternative to the existing (structuralist) approaches to EU foreign policy analysis.

Tomić draws on elements for his model predominantly from Vivien Schmidt's discursive institutionalism and Teun van Dijk's sociocognitive approach to critical discourse analysis. The model acknowledges a material reality outside socially constructed structures of meaning but posits three key layers of information processing and filtering: the global/societal level, the individual level and the group/organisational level. At each level of information processing, structures of meaning are created differently and agents have a greater or lesser degree of constraint or opportunity in their relation to existing structures. In the model, the assumption of discursive institutionalism of 'sentient agents', with background ideational abilities and foreground discursive abilities, is complemented by an intermediate step of cognition, namely preference formation. The societal and the organisational levels of information processing represent the constraining or enabling structures (background ideational abilities), which determine preference formation and subsequently the discursive action of the agent (foreground discursive abilities).

Maintaining the focus on the EU's foreign policy, the fifth article by Cristian Nițoiu explores the link between the various narratives constructed in relation to the EU's foreign policy and the way they unfold into policy practice. Narratives are seen here as overarching discursive categories which result from the overlapping of various discourses and tend to remain stable over time when shared by a certain political community. The article focuses on five narratives which are considered to dominate the way the EU chooses to engage with other actors in its external relations: EU as a security provider, EU as a democratizer and spreader of 'good' norms, EU as an actor that contributes to or assures global peace, EU as an entity that contributes to the well-being of peoples around the world and finally the narrative of EU good neighbourliness. Nițoiu suggests that all five narratives are characterized by a huge discrepancy between their underlying ambitious goals and aims and the way they are put into practice. Moreover, the EU is found to be aware of such discrepancies, always trying to downgrade the goals on which its narratives are predicated upon in order to match the policy failures that plague its external relations. While in the case of the security narrative the EU tries to overlook its poor policy outcomes altogether, other states such as the US or China are used as scapegoats in order to justify the Union's failure to effectively contribute to the well-being of peoples around the world. Niţoiu suggests that one solution for overcoming these discrepancies involve raising the level of willingness and political commitment of member states which would help develop the EU's resources and instruments in external relations.

The narrative of good neighbourliness highlighted by Niţoiu is analysed from another perspective and in a more comprehensive way by Vanda Amaro Dias. The sixth article by Dias examines the way the EU's and Russia's perceptions of each other shapes the way the Union chooses to engage with Moscow in its external relations. The article achieves this by analysing the way both Russia and the EU engage with the countries of and issues underlying the Eastern Neighbourhood. By employing a critical constructivist framework which underscores the links between discourse, interest and practices, and the way in which the former unfolds into the latter, Dias provides an insightful view into the way in which the EU's discursive self-image and perception of other actors (i.e. Russia) can shape its interest and policies. It can be argued that the EU and Moscow are inclined to cooperate as their discourses and subsequent mutual perceptions entrench them into a system of overlapping practices and interests in the Eastern Neighbourhood. Both discursively and in practice, their cooperation hinges upon a number of aspects, such as regional stabilization, economic development or security enhancement in their shared neighbourhood. On the other hand, the article reinforces the idea that Russia and the EU perceive each other in an antagonistic manner, due to the fact that both seem to desire to reinforce their internal security by increasing their regional and global influence.

Whether focusing on concrete policies or institutions or examining different theories, the contributions to this special issue map out and document the different ways in which discourse and discourse theory can shed new light on the development of the European project. Moreover, they explore a series of relevant policy areas where discursive approaches and discourse related theories can (and/or should) be successfully employed. In doing so, the special issue highlights a deep commitment to interdisciplinarity, while at the same time applying a range of perspectives in a consistent manner. However, the articles also show that there is still a long way before discourse would come to infiltrate and pervade the study of certain policy areas. Beyond the contributions in this special issue, the relationship between different types of discourses and narratives could shed even more light on the less mundane aspects of the political and institutional development of the European Union and its ambitions. Finally, one word of caution (or hopefulness?) should also be expressed here as a discursive turn might take hold of European Union studies and become the mainstream in the study of the European project. In this regard, it will be intriguing to observe the way in which new political developments, both internal and external to the European - such as the long lasting Euro zone crisis – will shape the amount of attention and focus that scholars will pay to discourse in the coming years.

References

Borzel, T. & Risse, T. (2007) Europeanization: The domestic impact of European Union Politics, in: K. E. Jorgensen, M. Pollack & B. J. Rosamond (Eds) *The Sage Handbook of European Union Politics,* pp. 484–504 (London: Sage).

Beland, D. (2009) Ideas, institutions, and policy change, *Journal of European Public Policy*, 16(5), pp. 701–718.

Carpentier, N. & De Cleen, B. (2007) Bringing discourse theory into media studies: The applicability of discourse theoretical analysis (DTA) for the study of media practises and discourses, *Journal of Language and Politics*, 6(2), pp. 265–293.

Checkel, J. T. & Katzenstein, P. J. (Eds) (2009) *European Identity* (Cambridge: Cambridge University Press).

Diez, T. (1999) Speaking 'Europe': The politics of integration discourse, *Journal of European Public Policy*, 6(4), pp. 598–613.

Diez, T. (2001) Europe as a Discursive Battleground, *Cooperation and Conflict*, 36(1), pp. 5–38.

Diez, T. (2005) Constructing the self and changing others: Reconsidering 'normative power Europe', *Millennium – Journal of International Studies*, 33(3), pp. 613–636.

Favell, A. & Guiraudon, V. (2009) The sociology of the European Union, *European Union Politics*, 10(4), pp. 550–576.

Featherstone, K. & Radaelli, C. M. (2003) *The Politics of Europeanization* (Oxford: Oxford University Press).

Goetz, K. H. & Hix, S. (2000) *Europeanised Politics? European Integration and National Political Systems* (London: Routledge).

Hay, C. & Rosamond, B. (2001) Globalization, European integration and the discursive construction of economic imperatives, *Journal of European Public Policy*, 9(2), pp. 147–167.

Howorth, J. (2004) Discourse, ideas, and epistemic communities in European security and defence policy, *West European Politics*, 27(2), pp. 211–234.

Jachtenfuchs, M., Diez, T., & Jung, S. (1998) Which Europe? Conflicting Models of a Legitimate European Political Order, *European Journal of International Relations*, 4(4), pp. 409–445.

Laclau, E. & Mouffe, C. (2001) *Hegemony and Socialist Strategy: Towards a radical democratic politics* (London: Verso Books).

Larsen, H. (1997) *Foreign Policy and Discourse Analysis: France, Britain and Europe* (London: Routledge).

Manners, I. (2002) Normative power Europe: A contradiction in terms?, *JCMS: Journal of Common Market Studies*, 40(2), pp. 235–258.

Manners, I. (2006) Normative power Europe reconsidered: Beyond the crossroads, *Journal of European Public Policy*, 13(2), p. 182.

Manners, I., (2010) Global Europa: Mythology of the European Union in world politics, *JCMS: Journal of Common Market Studies*, 48(1), pp. 67–87.

Olsen, J. P. (2002) The many faces of Europeanization, *Journal of Common Market Studies*, 40(5), pp. 921–952.

Parsons, C. (2010) Ideas, position, and supranationality, in: D. Beland & R. H. Cox (Eds) *Ideas and Politics in Social Science Research*, pp. 127–142 (Oxford: Oxford University Press).

Radaelli, C. M. & Schmidt, V. A. (2005) *Policy Change & Discourse in Europe* (London: Routledge).

Risse, T. (2000) 'Let's argue!' Communicative action in world politics, *International Organization*, 54(1), pp. 1–39.

Risse, T. (2009) Social constructivism and European integration, in: A. Wiener & T. Diez (Eds) *European Integration Theory*, pp. 159–176. (Oxford: Oxford University Press).

Rosamond, B. (2007) European integration and the social science of EU studies: The disciplinary politics of a sub-field, *International Affairs*, 83(2), pp. 231–252.

Rumford, C. & Murray, P. (2003) Globalization and the limitations of European integration studies: Interdisciplinary considerations, *Journal of Contemporary European Studies*, 11(1), pp. 85–93.

Schmidt, V. A. (2001) The politics of economic adjustment in France and Britain: When does discourse matter?, *Journal of European Public Policy*, 8(2), p. 247.

Schmidt, V. A. (2008) Discursive institutionalism: The explanatory power of ideas and discourse, *Annual Review of Political Science*, 11(1), pp. 303–326.

Schmidt, V. A. (2011) Speaking of change: Why discourse is key to the dynamics of policy transformation, *Critical Policy Studies*, 5(2), pp. 106–126.

Waever, O. (2001) Identity, communities and foreign policy: Discourse analysis as foreign policy theory, in: L. Hansen & O. Waever (Eds) *European Integration and National Identity: The challenge of the Nordic states*, pp. 20–49 (London: Routledge).

Waever, O. (2009) Discursive approaches, in: A. Wiener & T. Diez (Eds) *European Integration Theory*, pp. 197–216 (Oxford: Oxford University Press).

Making the Mythical European: Elucidating the EU's Powerful Integration Instrument of Discursive Identity Construction

S. ANNE BOSTANCI
School of Politics, University of Surrey, UK

ABSTRACT   *Drawing on Thomas Kuhn's seminal analysis, this article argues that mainstream EUropean integration theories such as neo-functionalism and intergovernmentalism are unified by underlying ontological, epistemological and methodological assumptions – thus – conform to the same scientific paradigm. This means that while opening up opportunities for study of some aspects of EUropean integration, simultaneous closure occurs so that other aspects remain under-explored. The value of identifying this effect is to enable researchers to sound out complementary approaches and paradigms to overcome said limitations and elicit new insights. Adopting a focus on discourse as a means, as well as identity formation as a form of integration, Eder's attempt to transcend transactionalism's omission to focus on content and functions rather than density of transactions is a laudable example of this endeavour. However, it can be argued that he reproduces several of the mainstream integration theories' paradigmatic assumptions. Flood's account of political myth goes beyond such limitations. Usefully supplemented by a structural rather than normative understanding of ideology and extended beyond historico-ideological content, this approach allows for the study of the identity-endowing and integrating function of implicitly or explicitly ideologically marked narratives that establish what it means to be EUropean. Although tentative steps towards this focus of study exist in EUropean studies, more rigorous theorising and extensive empirical research are needed.*

Introduction

Research themes such as 'challenging the mainstream in European studies' and 'critiquing integration theory' appear to be heralding the beginning of a long overdue self-reflexiveness in the field conventionally called European studies.[1] The former phrase is the overarching theme of a recent conference panel[2] as well as the present publication. The latter paraphrases the title of a research seminar at the Jean Monnet Centre of Excellence of a well-known London university.[3] The present article welcomes this self-reflexive turn and endeavours to contribute to it. However, self-reflexiveness may be taken further by posing questions as to what can be achieved by challenging and what comes after critiquing. Therefore, it is the aim of this article not only to contribute to the aforementioned challenge and critique, but also to make explicit what benefits can be reaped from such approaches and to illustrate in how far they are, not a passing fashion, but a substantive and important contribution to the field.

In order to do so, the article draws on the concept of the 'scientific paradigm' as developed by Thomas Kuhn (1970). The article argues that the mainstream theories of EUropean integration belong to the same paradigm, as a number of ontological, epistemological and methodological assumptions can be identified that they hold in common. The article further argues that while the paradigmatic assumptions and resulting theories, approaches and methods open up the opportunity to study certain aspects of the phenomenon, they simultaneously foreclose analysis of other aspects relevant to European integration. As such, they should be complemented by assumptions of another paradigm, which will allow for the exploration of structures and processes in European integration that have thus far been overlooked and neglected. For this reason, 'challenging the mainstream' in the present context does not refer to the calling into question of the utility of existing mainstream integration theories or for their abandonment altogether. Instead, it suggests challenging their hegemony and exclusive claim to validity and utility. This means, challenging here refers to complementing established theories and practices of analysis with different, innovative ones that will allow complementary insights. As a critical constructionist paradigm is considered the most fruitful in such an endeavour and the role of discourse has long been neglected in the field in question, the present article introduces a critical discourse analytical approach to making sense of an important aspect of the structures and processes of EUropean integration, namely EUropean identity. In this approach, critique – often misunderstood as motivated by Euro-sceptical or even anti-European sentiments – does not however refer to criticism of theoretical commitments or practical instruments of either governance or research. It refers to an endeavour to shed light on the question of how understandings and practices (have) come about and to highlight the structures and processes of power that allow(ed) them to do so in the current shape and form – a critical ontology of the present, for short.

The present article is structured into six sections. The first briefly outlines dominant mainstream integration theories and the debate between them. The second section offers a definition of the term paradigm and highlights the underlying assumptions that the previously discussed theories have in common, which justify their conceptualisation as belonging to the same paradigm. Third is a section that explains that the foundations of a different, innovative paradigm can be found in some scholarly engagement from within mainstream studies of EUropean integration. The fourth section sets out, in general terms, how a critical discursive constructionist approach overcomes the limitations of the paradigm identified and can, thus, complement it usefully to provide new insights into the process of EUropean integration. Fifth, the concept of 'political myth' is introduced to offer a specific conceptual framework that allows for the study of EUropean identity, which, in turn, is considered an important aspect of EUropean integration. Finally, the last section of the article outlines previous EUropean studies engagement with this concept, highlighting its shortcomings, and lists some examples of possible research material.

European Integration Theories

In order to outline in how far mainstream European integration theories belong to the same, in many respects limiting as well as enabling, paradigm, it is necessary to outline their basic tenets. Theoretical engagement with European integration has long been dominated by the on-going debate between neo-functionalism (Haas, 1958) and intergovernmentalism (Hoffmann, 1966; Moravscik, 1993). Despite the advent of other approaches, for instance concerned with forms and levels of governance (Marks et al., 1996) and policy networks (Petersen, 2009), these two theories take pre-eminence in a field much in thrall to classical notions of international relations (IR) theory. This may be due to the fact that they provide more coherent and easily instrumentalised theoretical frameworks than other theories – in other words: their ability to offer both grand explanations and facilitate empirical hypothesis-testing. They also both lend themselves to imply the support of one or the other normative standpoint of what the outcome of EUropean integration should be; continuing intergovernmental or increasingly supranational structures and processes.

Intergovernmentalism, in a nutshell, describes the European Union (EU) and its predecessors as mere conglomerations of states or organisations set up by an intergovernmental treaty, and emphasises the role and continuing relevance of the nation state in their structure, processes, internal mechanisms and external relations. It explains that nation states – understood, following the classical IR conceptualisation, as nominalised self-interested actors in the international system – only cooperate when it is in their interest. When this is the case, cooperation can take place, even on a large scale. However, in essence, their self-interest will not allow cooperation to take on its own dynamics of solidarity or habit, and will be discontinued if advantages for the state cease to be gained or if perceived disadvantages outweigh them.

In contrast, neo-functionalism aims to account for incremental processes of integration that express just such dynamics, claiming that they will culminate in the telos of a supranational European state or state-like structure. This theory has its foundations in practical plans to facilitate regional cooperation such as David Mitrany's functionalism and Jean Monnet's vision of his project of European integration, yet turns these into a theoretical framework for the study of integration (cf. Jo, 2007). It claims that by a process of 'spill-over' integration in one policy area will lead to integration in others. The areas most often envisioned to be affected in this way are the following: starting from the economic realm, initial spill-over will affect the political, and later ones lead to integration in the cultural realm (cf. Shore, 2000).

Some confirmation of this theory is often read from the fact that spill-over appears to have taken place from the economic to the political realm, e.g., in the formation, first, of the single market, and then, of Union citizenship. Nevertheless, it should be remembered that this is a theory and that validity in one area does not guarantee validity in another; therefore, spill-over into the cultural realm should not be taken for granted as it is by many EU officials and scholars. The danger is that a theory that appeals to so-called common sense is applied to an area in which processes are at work that are far too complex to be made sense of easily. What is commonly overlooked is the fact that spill-over from the economic to the political realm required mainly rationally driven political–legal action instigated by a small elite, while the spill-over to the social and cultural realms would require a (spontaneous or socially engineered) shift in a large number of individuals' affective attitudes and behaviour. And while claims have been made under this theory's banner about socialisation and changes in affective attitudes and behaviour of the political elites within the EU's institutions, it fails to account for how such a large-scale shift in ordinary individuals' identities may come about.

Instead, the theory carries an assumption of automaticity that led many – both European Union officials and scholars – to believe in the inevitability of the above-mentioned social and cultural spill-over and to overlook the fact that this very assumption obscured a lack of understanding of the nature and features of, as well as actors in processes of identification, socialisation, and the expression of belonging. Rather unsurprisingly, the failure of this process to manifest in practice has resulted in great incomprehension and lamentation. As a result, 'European identity' now figures largely in political and academic debate, both in terms of attempted affirmation versus negation of its existence (or even possibility) and in attempts to identify or devise theoretical and practical approaches to fostering it (e.g., by means of political rights and symbolic representation). Both the dominant integration theories have found it easy enough to include this issue in their overall approach. However, as neither of these theories engage in any detail with the question of how identities, cultural ones as well as quasi-national supranational ones, are formed, it can be seriously doubted that they will provide any useful insights into the question of the existence, emergence or even possibility of a EUropean identity.

The Paradigmatic Nature of Mainstream European Integration Theories

The lack of an understanding of such social processes as the development of a (shared) EUropean identity indicates that the mainstream EUropean integration theories can be made sense of as belonging to one and the same paradigm. For, the nature of paradigms is fundamentally bifurcated: on the one hand, they open up opportunities, indeed form the prerequisite, of postulating theories and testing hypotheses, which is why they are indispensable. On the other hand, as structural linguistics (De Saussure, 1983) explains, meaning is given to one paradigm[4] only through the exclusion or negation of others. Thus, scientific paradigms may open up some opportunities for study, but they necessarily simultaneously foreclose opportunities of knowledge generation in other directions. This is why it can only be of benefit to a discipline or field of study to allow and welcome the co-existence of multiple paradigms.

Forming a dominant paradigm, the mainstream integration theories combine foundational works (as indicated above) and they manage to account for or resonate with a number of (albeit, as pointed out above, not all) important points within the field. More importantly according to Kuhn's (1970) definition, they display an identifiable pattern of underlying ontological, epistemological and methodological assumptions that pose as 'rules' of the paradigm's 'language game' (Wittgenstein, 2001). These rules do not imply that the field may not display a number of different approaches, foci of study and research questions, but that all these are unified by the basic assumptions that researchers hold in common. Constituting the scientific community that adheres to them, these paradigmatic assumptions determine scientific practice and thinking; amongst others, they permeate researchers' theoretical commitments; they provide hegemonic, normalised – yet inherently selective and contestable – definitions, units of analysis, methodological preferences.

Despite being hegemonic and normalised, the underlying paradigmatic assumptions can be uncovered through studying the patterns of the 'language game'. Such an analysis exposes the fact that the mainstream theories exhibit significant oversights as well as inconsistencies between the ontology, epistemology and methodology conventionally drawn on and the phenomenon they are aiming to account for. This is to say that, in the present context, the problems that European integration poses take shapes or display features that are, at least in part, incommensurable with the theories that claim to explain them. The oversight relevant for this article has already been identified as regarding an understanding of processes of EUropean identification as a form of EUropean integration. Therefore, attention will now be drawn in more detail to some aspects of the existing paradigm that – while unifying across different integration theories – hinder progress in furthering such an understanding.

Firstly, nation states or state-like structures and nominalised national or supranational institutions and decision making processes usually form the focus of study in the context of studies of the EU. This expresses an exclusive methodological nationalism, which is considered to be erroneous. When trying to make sense of identity, the human being – both as an individual and in groups – and his or her identity – both on the psychological and the sociological level – must be paid due attention as a separate and valid unit of study. Secondly, the states or state-like structures mentioned are commonly portrayed in an essentialist and post-Enlightenment (quasi-)individualistic and rationalistic light. It is argued here, that both essentialism and (quasi-)individualism and rationalism as assumptions about the nature of states or supranational institutions are mistaken as regards to their exclusivity. They should be complemented by an acknowledgement and improved understanding that collective and affective attitudes and behaviours are of great importance in politics and international relations in general and in constructions of identity in particular. Thirdly, states and state-like structures in EUropean studies are usually made sense of through a theoretical commitment to the notion of historical evolution. This includes the conceptual complex of history–teleology–inevitability. Yet it is argued here that while a focus on historical events or developments may offer some insights into EUropean identity, its exclusivity is unnecessarily limiting. It is so, for two reasons: firstly, historical determinism is an oversimplification of processes of identity construction and, secondly, it obscures aspects of structural and discursive power that impact on identities and processes of identity construction, which do not fit into classic IR understandings and the above-outlined paradigmatic assumptions.

Foundations of an Alternative Paradigm

It is interesting to note in this context that, while these hegemonic paradigmatic assumptions largely go unquestioned amongst integration theorists and scholars adhering to one or the other schools of thought that conform to the paradigm, self-reflexivity could easily have been achieved in the field of European integration studies. Alternative approaches already existed among early theoretical endeavours to make sense of European integration. Transactionalism (Deutsch, 1953) – a school of thought overshadowed by the long-established and vehement debate of the two previously mentioned theories and thus marginalised as an integration theory – offered tools for the study of EUropean integration in non-rationalistic, particularistic, transactionalist and non-normative terms from its early days. Furthermore, it has been directly concerned with issues closely associated with EUropean identity all along. It focuses on the conditions necessary for political integration to occur and identifies relevant aspects not only in shared political and administrative institutions, but also in shared communication and extended mutual transactions of individuals. In all these, it emphasises mutual responsiveness as the key to the establishment of a sense of community or 'we-feeling' among the populations of the integrating region. And while initial studies following this school of thought were overly concerned with the quantitative dimension, e.g., measuring the density of transaction processes, the theory emphasised from the start that such an integration project depended on more qualitative aspects such as complex and long-term processes of social learning, often over generations, in which shared symbols, identities, habits of cooperation, memories, values and norms would lead a group of individuals to consider themselves a people. For this reason, it has received increasing attention in recent years.

Eder (2007) builds on this theory and emphasises the transactionalist nature of communication. In a move akin to Hobsbawm's (1983) theory of the invention of tradition, he describes shared stories as formative of a 'communication space'. Amongst these shared identity-endowing stories, he identifies two types in particular in the EUropean communication space: those referring to the experience of fairness springing from the fact that rules of membership of the EU are based on a legal contract and therefore the same for all members,[5] and those referring to historical events that are perceived to be shared (in the widest sense of commonly attributing significance, of whatever kind, to them). Following Weber (1956), Eder refers especially to such stories that refer to common existential experiences, such as struggles for life and death. However, in his emphasis on such historical at the expense of other identity-endowing narratives, he reproduces the evolutionary understanding including assumptions of teleology and inevitability, which is characteristic of the paradigm identified in the previous section. Simultaneously, the emphasis on legal equality (or perceptions thereof) suggests that he also subscribes to the paradigmatic rationalistic and quasi-individualistic ideas of self-interest identified above. Moreover, while Eder first refers to the possibility of individual identification, large parts of his article seem to be referring not to individuals but to states as actors. In all these respects, an opportunity is lost to fundamentally challenge and substantially complement the existing paradigm, despite the fact that Eder's move to a focus on communication as a social and identity-endowing practice holds the key to a more innovative approach to the study of European integration, namely that of discursive construction.

Studying Discourse: Complementing the Mainstream Paradigm

While social constructionist approaches[6] have found their way into EUropean studies in parallel to their gradual acceptance in the field of international relations in general, discursive approaches are still scarce and have certainly not penetrated the mainstream of integration theories; rare examples of such engagement with the EU usually spring from other disciplines, e.g., linguistics (see Cramer, 2010). Yet, understanding processes of social construction, and, as a subcategory of it, discursive construction, not only provides insights that complement those offered by mainstream theories of European integration, but it provides insights that are logically prior to those that conventional approaches can elicit, as well as powerfully political in that they allow identification of the structural conditions and relations of power that allow meanings to take shape. The argument goes as follows: constructionist approaches, in contrast to traditional positivist ones, hold that reality is not a given 'out there' but that its meaning arises from humans' interactions.[7] One, and the most important, such interaction is discourse. Discourse includes, but goes beyond mere written texts and utterances or conversations; it also refers to the malleable, yet durable, structures of what is considered acceptable and comprehensible form and to established contents and structures of meaning. For instance, the EU is constructed by means of its constitutive discourses both in terms of what is and what can be said in and about it and what is acceptable to say about it. So is EUropean identity. The argument in favour of analysis of discursive construction then is that, instead of taking for granted the nature of the EU and studying it with descriptive methods, it makes it possible to ask questions about how it (has) come to mean what it is widely understood to mean. Such 'how-possible questions' (Doty, 1993) regarding the emergence of established 'meanings-in-use' (Weldes, 1998) surrounding the EU are logically prior to those posed (and sometimes answered) by studies conforming to the mainstream paradigm in the sense that the formation of meanings precedes any of the aspects that theories that take meanings for granted can ever study.

One area in which 'how-possible questions' can illuminate 'meanings-in-use' concerns established and emerging meanings of EUropean identity. Rather than assuming the form (national or quasi-national, singular rather than multiple) and content (usually ethno-cultural and linguistic) that identities take and attempting to identify or foster these in so-called European identity, this approach allows researchers to study the discursive processes that give rise to and establish as 'fact' those forms and contents and to identify the power relations that underlie them. The approach also enables study of the substantive constituents of the meaning of the term 'EUropean', which is an 'empty signifier' (Laclau & Mouffe, 2001). As such, it acts as an umbrella term that ties together a variety of concepts and, by doing so in a particular way, offers them a collective morphology that only in its entirety signifies the meaning of the term. In order to study such meanings, it is necessary to study the discursive contents and patterns that give rise to them.

However, the paradigm represented by the mainstream integration theories features several assumptions and foci of study that make such study impossible. It implies a teleology that obscures contradictions and the operation of power within the integration process (which include the common use – in academia as elsewhere – of the term Europe as synonymous with EU); it assumes that politics and identity construction can be made sense of in rationalistic terms of administration and cognitive self-interest rather than affect (fear, aspirations, pride, etc), and in terms of individualism rather than collectivity. Intentional or not, these assumptions lead to a necessarily theory- or method-driven approach, such as 'European identity is X; is it possible to achieve X and how so?' Discourse analysis, in contrast, allows for an approach that starts with the problem 'What is European identity?' complemented with the question 'How is it possible (by what internal structures and patterns of meaning) that EUropean identity has come to refer/ refers to its current meaning?' Thus, a focus on discursive construction belongs to a different paradigm that can usefully complement the mainstream one in a variety of areas of study relevant to EUropean integration, for instance policy matters such as enlargement, education, security, external relations, etc (cf. various articles in this publication).

As mentioned above, 'how-possible questions' do not only elicit the actual means of the social (and discursive) construction of reality. They can also be used as a critical starting point to identify and explore the power structures that facilitate this process, which, in turn, may open up opportunities to find remedies to problems caused by current practices and faced by the institutions in question. While power is certainly an object of study in the realm of international relations in general and sometimes also in that of European integration, it is understood differently in social and discursive constructionist accounts; the latter aim to identify structures and practical examples of the exercise of power, not to influence decisions or coerce people or states into specific behaviours but to determine meanings. Strategies of such power include establishing 'common sense', obscuring contradictions, allowing or disallowing discursive participation based on identity or social position of the speaker or content of speech, processes of nominalisation and predication, and the like. They can be identified by means of deconstruction, i.e., juxtaposition against (existing or possible) alternative discourses, which does away with the assumption of inevitability. It is the resulting opportunity for critical reflexion, which may round out well-disposed accounts of European integration, that a complementary paradigm and the method of critical discourse analysis are valuable.

A Focus on Political Myth: Expression of a Complementary Paradigm

Such reflexivity as well as the added insights offered by the method of discourse analysis are particularly valuable in the area of 'social learning and normative diffusion' – thus far under-explored in the context of studies of the EU (Checkel, 1999, p. 546). 'Social learning and normative diffusion' can, of course, be seen to form a parallelism to the 'identity formation and ideological discourse' discussed in the present article. It can be argued that the former is brought about by the latter. Thus it is instructive to study identity-endowing ideological narratives (including, but going beyond those identified by Eder and discussed above); namely, 'political myths' (Flood, 2002).

The defining features of political myths – which can be understood as a form of political discourse in the mundane and the Foucauldian sense simultaneously – according to Flood (ibid.), are, firstly, that they are narratives that carry ideological beliefs; secondly, that they present themselves as and are held to be true and, often, sacred or sacrosanct and, thus, insulated from critique; thirdly, they may appear in diachronic variations and synchronic (e.g., regional) analogies. All these characteristics are accepted here, including the premise of the first feature of political mythis and its structural understanding of ideology. The understanding adopted here is described by Freeden (1996) and defines ideologies as 'patterns of thought-behaviour' or clusters of concepts that give meaning to the world in empirical and normative terms and, thus, enable individual and, more importantly, collective action – and, simultaneously as a basis of and with it, identification. Here, the individualism and quasi-individualism of the mainstream paradigm of European integration theory is overcome. This is helpful, for identification of the kind that is discussed cannot be understood in terms of the individual alone. However, a forth defining characteristic proposed by Flood (2002), namely that myths display, in their narrative, a sequence of connected past, present and/or future events, is considered as unnecessarily limiting in its insistence in a temporal or historical reference point. It is, therefore, replaced by the understanding simply that a constant reference point is needed around which a narrative is constructed. It is true that historical events are frequently mobilised as constant reference points in political myths.[8] However, other constant reference points also figure largely; e.g., antagonistic relations with an 'other' or 'out-group', or ethical ideals. Finally, to return to Flood's defining features, it should be noted that although myth is often understood in common parlance as referring to a story untrue or fictional even if it is more or less widely believed, such an understanding of necessary inaccuracy is considered mistaken here, for it has no bearing on the identity-endowing function of a mythopoeic narrative discourse.

In their combination, these criteria carry a variety of important points. It has already been stated that they enable collective action, but it is worthwhile to look at this in detail. By relating ideological content by means of narratives, myths provide inspiration and justification that can form the basis of any kind of human action; they can express a will to act or condone inaction and quietism. As such, MacNeill (1986, p. 23) claims:

> ... myth lies at the basis of human society. That is because myths are general statements about the world and its parts, and in particular about nations and other human in-groups, that are believed to be true and then acted on whenever circumstances suggest or require common response. This is mankind's substitute for instinct. It is the unique and characteristic human way of acting together. A people without a full quiver of relevant agreed-upon statements, accepted in advance through education or less formalized acculturation, soon finds itself in deep trouble, for, in the absence of believable myths, coherent public action becomes very difficult to improvise or sustain.

While not specifically concerned with political myth, this assessment already suggests the political function of mythical narratives in general. More politically oriented analyses have identified myth as the 'ideologically marked' (Flood, 2002) or 'value-impregnated beliefs and notions that men [sic]... live by and live for' (MacIver, 1947, p. 4). They 'turn valuations into propositions about the nature of things' (ibid., p. 39) and without the direction they provide no political action could be taken. As the above analogy to instinct suggests, in their narrative form, myths work beyond and, thus, defy rational argument as the dominant form of political expression (Sorel, 1999; Bottici, 2007). Here, it becomes clear how an approach that proposes study of this particular type of discourse can overcome the paradigmatic limitation to rationalism that mainstream integration theories and studies of the European Union display. However, the study of political myth does not imply an analytically unhelpful endorsement of (alleged) irrationality. Rather, it draws attention to role of the affective dimension in communication, identification and politics in general. Particularly in combination with Mouffe's (1998) argument that de-ideologising and de-politicising politics, which often involves the dismissal of its affective dimension, leads to – literally – disaffection and apathy, this is an important observation to keep in mind, especially in the apparently legitimacy crisis-ridden European Union. In this respect too, allowing an alternative paradigm to complement the mainstream one, can only be of advantage to the field of EUropean studies, as identifying room for improvement and mechanisms to achieve it may offer solutions to problems that the Union is currently facing.[9]

On a more abstract level, located at the intersection of political science, anthropology and sociology, drawing on the concept of political myth is not only theoretically enriching and empirically illuminating but also methodologically sound; it is in line with the understanding that EUropean integration is a political as well as cultural phenomenon. The concept overcomes the compartmentalisation of disciplines – a move so necessary in view of the fact that the world out there, albeit constructed, does not conform to disciplinary and paradigmatic boundaries. This means that it becomes possible to study aspects of identity in general and quasi-national and EUropean identity in particular that were formerly taken for granted. Features conventionally mobilised in EUropean studies for the definition of such forms of identity are linguistic similarity, essentialised (sometimes even assumedly primordial) ethnic background, community of fate, ideological (religious, political, etc) unity, and so forth. However, while studies of national identity have long identified these as socially discursively constructed or 'imagined' (Anderson, 1983), in the context of studies of the European Union, essentialist understandings still hold some currency. This can be deduced from the continued conviction that lack of linguistic similarity and shared ethnic background are problematic. Furthermore, due to the dominance of the paradigm outlined above, the constructedness of the history and telos of its community of fate as well as its implicit as well as explicit ideological make-up, its worldview, ethics, and characteristic 'repertoires of evaluation' (Delanty & Rumford, 2005), have been overlooked. The complementary approach suggested here allows insights into them all, for they are constructed in narratives or, more precisely, political myths.

Taking EUropean Studies (and Studies of EUropean Myths) Further

It is important to note here, that initial steps in the study of the EU's political myths have been taken. Some writers have touched on political myth-making of the European Union yet broadly remained in thrall to historiography (Stråth, 2005), while others have identified interesting aspects of the EU's language game (e.g., that it, too, like the field that is dedicated to its study, relies overly on rationalism; Hansen & Williams, 1999). Again others (Jo, 2007) have identified the significance of political myths in times of political crisis to mobilise we-feelings and rally support for particular solutions, but overlook its equal significance (though invisibility due to success) at times of political equilibrium. Finally, in early 2010, the *Journal of Common Market Studies* published a special issue (Della Sala, 2010) on the topic of European political myths. While a number of innovative ideas are presented by some (for example, one of the articles (Lenschow & Sprungk, 2010) dispensed with the evolutionary historical notion of myth), several of the articles regrettably miss the opportunity to engage in depth with definitional questions, paradigmatic assumptions, theoretical commitments, methodological considerations or critical analysis of the EU narratives they discuss. As a result, academic engagement thus far (especially this recent example) may be vulnerable to the criticism of mainly recounting the EU's policy discourses rather than analysing their function as political myth. Furthermore, some articles reproduce conventional paradigmatic theoretical and methodological commitments, e.g., methodological nationalism and quasi-individualism (see Jones, 2010; Smismans, 2010) or a sole focus on historical memory (see Hansen-Magnusson & Wiener, 2010), that limit their insights. Most importantly, the relevance of the concept to issues of identity (and legitimacy) as well as the ideological nature of myth that is at the basis of its identity-endowing function are overlooked altogether. As a result, the particular EUropean identity promoted by the Union's myths, which (potentially) contributes to the process of integration, also remains unquestioned and unstudied.

This means that more thorough as well as critical study of the EU's political myths is required. Ideologically marked, affective and identity-endowing narratives are ubiquitous in discourses of and around the European Union. They can be found in a variety of EU policy discourses, e.g., those of citizenship, enlargement, environmental or social policy, and its external relations through trade and development aid. They can also be found in a myriad of sources: various institutions – foremost the Commission as it is the most proactive amongst the EU institutions in the fields of political agenda-setting and marketing – and texts such as the treaties, declarations, policy papers, inter- and intra-institutional communications, and public relations brochures.[10] By means of critical discourse analysis(including semiotic analysis to enable study of images as well as text),meaning-endowing ideological tenets can be extracted from these texts. These may refer to both the nature and aspirations of the Union or integration project *per se* and the self-understandings it offers its citizens as EUropean, i.e., mythical representations of the EUropean(s).

Concluding Remarks

A little over a decade ago, Christiansen, Jørgensen and Wiener found fault with studies of the European Union in that 'there is a certain paradox in that what is often referred to as *la construction européenne* has not received any systematic attention from constructivist scholars' (Christiansen et al., 2001, p. 1). It is interesting that these authors seem to assume that blame lies with academics, when this phenomenon and the overwhelming dominance of the mainstream paradigm described here can also be suggested to be the result of structural power by making reference to the improbability of the allocation of research funding, which in this field is to a substantial part provided by the EU, to studies featuring an overtly critical approach. Attempting to identify the culprit in this way, however, is beside the point. What is of importance is to identify the problem. A number of scholars have taken up the challenge to remedy it since the above-quoted publication. However, a rigorous understanding of the difficulties involved is lacking. As the discussion above suggests, it is due mainly to the fact that the paradigmatic assumptions that mainstream theories of EUropean integration share foreclose the possibility of rigorous problem-driven study that social and discursive constructionist analysis of the EU is proving to be such a difficult task. It is argued here that, with regard to EUropean identity, a focus on the ideologically marked, affective discursive processes of political myth-making and myth-dissemination is the most fruitful.

To recapitulate, the argument developed in the present article is this: mainstream European integration theories such as neo-functionalism and intergovernmentalism share underlying ontological, epistemological and methodological assumptions, i.e., they conform to the same scientific paradigm. While opening up opportunities for analysis of some aspects of EUropean integration, these paradigmatic assumptions simultaneously make the study of other aspects impossible. When looking at the nature and processes of construction of EUropean identity, a critical social constructionist approach is needed to complement the former paradigm. While an instructive attempt at studying the discourses that give rise to EUropean identity exists, it does not go far enough. For this reason the concept of political myth is drawn on, as it accounts for the structural ideological, affective and individual as well as collective identity-endowing dimensions of political discourse. It also enables critical how-possible questions about current meanings-in-use. And while the concept of political myth has been discussed within EUropean studies before, these previous engagements are still guided by the paradigmatic assumptions of mainstream integration theories in many respects, they offer limited insight into the nature and functions of political myths in the context of the European Union and they overlook completely the relevance of the concept to EUropean identity. As such, the present article is an appeal for more rigorous theorising and extensive empirical research.

Notes

1. All references to European studies, European integration and European integration theories, as well as European identity are used here with caution due to the fact that the terms are conventional ones that do not draw attention to the fact that most studies in this field, the processes described as integration and by means of integration theory, as well as the identity understood as European are concerned not with a wide conceptual–geographical notion of Europe, but mainly with the European Union. In order to avoid contributing to the normalising effect that uncritical use of these terms has, and the resulting unquestioning perpetuation of the 'colonisation of Europe' by the European Union (Boedeltje & van Houtum, 2008), the terms EUropean studies, EUropean integration, EUropean integration theory and EUropean identity are used in this article.
2. UACES Student Forum conference 'New frontiers in European studies', held at the University of Surrey, Guildford, UK, on 30 June and 1 July 2011.
3. Research seminar held at King's College London on 26 January 2011 under the title 'A contribution to the critique of integration theory'. The speaker was Magnus Ryner from Oxford Brookes University. His critique mainly involved exposing said established set of theories as a paradigm from the perspective of international political economy. Drawing inspiration from that presentation, the author's combined interest in EUropean identity, Wittgenstein's concept of 'language games' and in discursive construction more generally, which had made it clear that mainstream integration theories were both limited in their insights and conformed to rules of their own, led to this article.
4. Here the term refers to the grammatical function of a word rather than a scientific paradigm, but it is no coincidence that the term is the same, for both refer to a relationship of alternative rather than complementarity – be it of words in linguistic structures or scientific paradigms in meaning structures that enable knowledge generation.
5. He overlooks, however, that the contractual nature of these rules does not overcome the arbitrariness of criteria of eligibility for membership.
6. Here it may be of advantage to draw readers' attention to the often ill-understood, related yet distinct, nature of social constructionism and social constructivism. Social constructionism can be seen to refer to an ontological outlook, a sociological conception of 'reality', 'world' (Kuhn, 1970) or 'imaginary' (see Calhoun, 2002) that social interaction affords meaning or gives rise to. In contrast, social constructivism can be understood as epistemological in nature and referring to individuals' psychological, cognitive processes in constructing concepts and understandings that enable them to make sense of and, in turn, act in the 'world'. Clearly, these two processes are closely linked in practice in a relationship of mutual contingency and continuous debate, affirmation or adaptation.
7. Attention is drawn here to a useful distinction regarding social construction. It is explained in an early attempt by Diez (2001) to outline the uses of the social constructionist approach to studies of the EU: Constructive realism assumes that, even though constructed, there is a world or reality 'out there'. In contrast to classical positivist approaches, however, it cannot be directly observed and made sense of, but can only be known or made knowable by means of the meaning systems of language (i.e., discursive social interaction). Constructive idealism, in contrast, assumes that it is the fact that there are actors engaged in the linguistic construction of reality that brings it into being.
8. In this guise, myths are similar to so-called historical memories of the past, which is the reason that the latter have received so much attention in the context of studies of national or quasi-national identities. However, the innocent notion of historical memories or historiography is misleading as ideological marking necessarily happens when such narratives are mobilised for political purposes. For this reason the term myth is chosen here.
9. Some may argue that this is not the point of academic work, but in view of the fact that a lot of academic engagement with the European Union is actively engaged in or lends itself to legitimising it, this cannot be considered a problematic proposition.
10. A research project on the latter is currently in progress.

References

Anderson, B. (1983) *Imagined Communities* (London, UK: Verso).
Boedeltje, F. & van Houtum, H. (2008) The abduction of Europe: A plea for less 'unionism' and more Europe, *Tijdschrift voor Economische en Sociale Geografie*, 99(3), pp. 361–365.

Bottici, C. (2007) *A Philosophy of Political Myth* (Cambridge, UK: Cambridge University Press).
Calhoun, C. (2002) Imagining solidarity: Cosmopolitanism, constitutional patriotism, and the public sphere, *Public Culture*, 14(1), pp. 147–151.
Checkel, J. T. (1999) Social construction and integration, *Journal of European Public Policy*, 6(4), pp. 545–546.
Christiansen, T., et al. (2001) *The Social Construction of Europe* (London, UK: Sage Publications).
Cramer, J. (2010) 'Do we really want to be like them?' Indexing Europeanness through pronominal use, *Discourse & Society*, 21(6), pp. 619–637.
Delanty, G. & Rumford, C. (2005) *Rethinking Europe* (Abingdon, UK: Routledge).
Della Sala, V. (Ed.) (2010) Political myth, mythology and the European Union, *Journal of Common Market Studies*, 48(1), pp. 1–190.
De Saussure, F. (1983) *Course in General Linguistics*, (La Salle, IL: Open Court).
Deutsch, K. (1953) *Nationalism and Social Communication. An Inquiry into the Foundations of Nationality* (Cambridge, MA: MIT Press).
Diez, T. (2001) Speaking "Europe": The politics of integration discourse, in: T. Christiansen et al. (Eds) *The Social Construction of Europe* (London, UK: Sage Publications) pp. 85–100.
Doty, R. L. (1993) Foreign policy as social construction: A post-positivist analysis of US counterinsurgency policy in the Philippines, *International Studies Quarterly*, 37(3), pp. 297–320.
Eder, K. (2007) Europa alsbesondererKommunikationsraum. ZurFrage der sozialen Integration einerkulturellheterogenenGesellschaft, *Berliner Journal fürSoziologie*, 17(1), pp. 33–50.
Flood, C. G. (2002) *Political Myth: A theoretical introduction* (London, UK: Routledge).
Freeden, M. (1996) *Ideologies and Political Theory* (Oxford, UK: Clarendon Press).
Haas, E. (1958) *The Uniting of Europe: Political, Social, and Economic Forces 1950–57* (Stanford, CA: Stanford University Press).
Hansen, L. & Williams, M. C. (1999) The myths of Europe: Legitimacy, community and the "crisis" of the EU, *Journal of Common Market Studies*, 37(2), pp. 233–249.
Hansen-Magnusson, H. & Wiener, A. (2010) Studying contemporary constitutionalism: Memory, myth and horizon, *Journal of Common Market Studies*, 48(1), pp. 21–44.
Hobsbawm, E. (1983) Introduction, in: E. Hobsbawm & T. Ranger (Eds) *The Invention of Tradition*, pp. 1–14 (Cambridge, UK: Cambridge University Press).
Hoffmann, S. (1966) Obstinate or obsolete? The fate of the nation state and the case of Western Europe, *Daedalus*, 95(3), pp. 862–915.
Jo, S.-S. (2007) *European Myth* (Langham, MD: University Press of America).
Jones, E. (2010) The economic mythology of European integration, *Journal of Common Market Studies*, 48(1), pp. 89–109.
Kuhn, T. (1970) *The Structure of Scientific Revolutions* (Chicago, IL: University of Chicago Press).
Laclau, E. & Mouffe, C. (1985) *Hegemony and Socialist Strategy* (London, UK: Verso).
Lenschow, A. & Sprungk, C. (2010) The myth of a green Europe, *Journal of Common Market Studies*, 48(1), pp. 133–154.
MacIver, R. M. (1947) *The Web of Government* (New York: The Macmillan Company).
MacNeill, W. H. (1986) *Mythistory and Other Essays* (Chicago, IL: University of Chicago Press).
Marks, G., et al. (1996) *Governance in the European Union* (London, UK: Sage Publications).
Moravscik, A. (1993) Preferences and power in the European Community. A liberal intergovernmentalist approach, *Journal of Common Market Studies*, 39(2), pp. 221–244.
Mouffe, C. (1998) The radical centre: A politics without adversary, *Soundings*, 9, pp. 11–23.
Petersen, J. (2009) Policy networks, in: A. Wiener & T. Diez, *European Integration Theory*, pp. 105–124 (Oxford, UK: Oxford University Press).
Shore, C. (2000) *Building Europe: The cultural politics of European integration* (London: Routledge).
Smismans, S. (2010) The European Union's fundamental rights myth, *Journal of Common Market Studies*, 48(1), pp. 45–66.
Sorel, G. (1999) *Reflections on Violence* (Cambridge, UK: Cambridge University Press).
Stråth, B. (2005) Methodological and substantive remarks on myth, memory and history in the construction of a European community, *German Law Journal*, 6(2), pp. 255–271.
Weber, M. (1956) *Wirtschaft und Gesellschaft: Grundriss der Verstehenden Soziologie* (Tübingen, Germany: Mohr).
Weldes, J. (1998) Bureaucratic politics: A critical constuctivist assessment, *International Studies Review*, 42(2), pp. 216–225.
Wittgenstein, L. (2001) *Philosophical Investigations* (Malden, UK: Blackwell).

The Battle Against Unfair Trade in the EU Trade Policy: A Discourse Analysis of Trade Protection

JOSUÉ F. MATHIEU* & SHARON WEINBLUM**
*FNRS Research Fellow, Université libre de Bruxelles
**Postdoctoral Research Fellow, Harvard University

ABSTRACT *The European Union considers Trade Defence Instruments (i.e., anti-dumping, countervailing duties and safeguards) as a cornerstone of the EU trade policy in the battle against 'unfair competition from across the globe'. At the same time, the rationale behind these instruments, or the fight against 'unfair trade practices', remains somehow woolly. In this article, we argue that it is crucial to unpack the different meanings bestowed on the concept of unfair trade. An interpretative perspective is therefore adopted in order to highlight the complexity behind this notion. The analysis is based on a systematic analysis of the debates revolving around the issue of Trade Defence Instruments held within the European Parliament during the current legislative session. First, we show that a specific storyline on unfair trade can be considered dominant. Second, we expose the 'kaleidoscopic' reality behind unfair trade, showing that this notion is a floating signifier. Against this backcloth, the article puts forward the argument that the institutionalisation of Trade Defence Instruments precisely relies on this character of unfair trade as a floating signifier.*

Introduction

Fairness is an ominous concept in debates regarding international trade. Labels such as 'Fairtrade', 'Fairtrade Max Havelaar', 'Oxfam', 'World Fair Trade Organization', or 'Fair Trade Certified', have become familiar to many consumers around the globe. These labels echo concerns about the need to offer a 'fair' compensation to producers, especially in poor countries. Lesser known to the broad public, fairness in international trade also refers in policy circles to concerns about the relation between domestic and foreign producers. Fairness in this case pertains to the ability to compete on an equal footing, or, to follow the sport metaphor usually used, to compete on a 'level playing field' (Cass & Boltuk, 1997). Specific trade policy instruments were therefore developed in the course of the twentieth century in order to fight 'unfair trade' from foreign producers

(Lowenfeld, 2008). Those instruments – collectively called trade remedies – include provisory duties (i.e., border taxes) imposed on foreign goods, either to fight the dumping of low cost goods (anti-dumping), to fight subsidised goods (countervailing duties), or to fight a sudden surge in imports (safeguards). While usually referred to as 'trade remedies', these instruments are collectively called 'trade defence instruments' within the European Union (EU), and the agency in charge of their implementation is the European Commission.

The European Commission considers trade defence instruments as a cornerstone of the European trade policy. 'Trade defence instruments are part of the multilateral system', says the European Commission in the communication *Global Europe*, 'and (they) help ensure that the benefits of openness are not undermined by unfair pricing, trading practices or subsidisation' (EU Commission, 2006). Symbolising this role played by trade defence instruments, the EU Commission's web page on trade defence instruments and documentation on the subject harbour a shield surrounded by the 12 stars of the European flag. Trade defence instruments are therefore regarded as crucial in order to 'ensure that international trade rules are fully respected' and to 'maintain a level playing field' (Karel De Gucht, European Commissioner for Trade, European Commission, 2011). EU Commissioner De Gucht expressed at many occasions that trade defence instruments were at the very core of EU trade policy. And discourse is followed by action.

Between 1995 and 2011 the European Union was third, after India and the United States, in the number of anti-dumping investigations launched (437 investigations, against respectively 656 and 458) and second, after the United States, in the number of countervailing investigations (61 against 114) (WTO, 2012).[1] Some of these cases have become high-profile because of special attention in the media, others because of tense economic relations induced by the imposition of duties. This was notably the case when the EU imposed duties on shoes from China and Vietnam, following an investigation in 2005. The recent launch in September 2012 of an investigation into solar panels from China (EU Commission, 2012b) might well lead to a similar dynamic of escalation and retaliation with this country.

The wide use of trade remedies has long been criticised by economists. In the case of anti-dumping, for instance, most of them consider that current anti-dumping laws authorise a bad instrument, which poorly addresses its alleged target (Hoekman & Kostecki, 2001, pp. 317–330). The law of the World Trade Organization (WTO) offers the possibility to impose duties on dumped goods, i.e., goods imported in the country at a price 'less than the normal value', which is determined either on the basis of the home price or the cost of production (*this is the international law definition of dumping*). Economists dispute the need to fight dumping as defined by the WTO. According to them, anti-dumping should be limited to the fight of predatory pricing, a practice consisting in selling a product under the cost of production in order to drive foreign competitors out of business (*this is the economic definition of dumping*). This justification for resorting to anti-dumping duties dates back to the early twentieth century, at a time when the renowned economist Jacob Viner warned against low cost imports from Germany, which aimed, according to him, at killing international competitors. The problem, economists explain, is that predatory pricing is a demanding business practice, for predatory competitors would need both a sanctuary market (a closed market where it is impossible to re-import the dumped goods) and monopoly power in this market. To put it in the words of Mavroidis et al., 'Predation is not easy. It is a war' (Mavroidis et al., 2008, p.12). In this perspective, what economists regard as a legitimate rationale for anti-dumping has nothing to do with the rationale of anti-dumping laws and the actual target of anti-dumping.

In this article, we propose a new perspective on the rationale behind anti-dumping and trade remedies through an analysis of contemporary discourse on trade remedies. We are therefore less interested in the historical roots of antidumping than in contemporary discursive articulations. Our attention focuses on one particular locus: the European Parliament (EP). The European Parliament has indeed become an unavoidable player in European decision-making, since the attribution of co-decision over the shaping of trade remedy rules; the current reforms implementing the Treaty of Lisbon might actually give the EP even more power over these issues. The discourse about trade remedies in this forum has therefore started to truly matter. This discourse is furthermore reflective of concerns sparking from a broad political spectrum, which makes it particularly interesting to study. In particular, this article looks at the discursive articulations of notions such as anti-dumping, unfair trade and related topics present in the Members of the European Parliament's (MEPs) discourse. By studying discourse, the article shows that the notion of unfair trade plays a key role in the discursive articulations on trade remedies. We argue that the kaleidoscopic character of *unfair trade* finds an explanation in the fact that it is a floating signifier, around which actors rally. The analysis thus looks at the *chains of equivalence* linking unfair trade to other signifiers, i.e., the way this notion is discursively constructed in opposition to other signifiers. We further argue that this feature of *unfair trade* is crucial for understanding the extremely low level of contestation over anti-dumping and other trade remedies. This implies that the character of a signifier as floating might be crucial for the institutionalisation of trade policy instruments.

The following section displays our approach to discourse and explains the key theoretical concepts used in this article. Then, two sections apply this theoretical framework to the discourse on unfair trade in the European Parliament. The first one studies the dominant storyline about unfair trade present in the European Parliament; the second one studies the meanings given to the 'floating signifier' of unfair trade. These sections show that theoretical concepts such as 'storyline', 'floating signifier' or 'chain of equivalence' are extremely useful in order to understand the staunch consensus over anti-dumping. The conclusion discusses the main findings about the discursive articulations at play and reflects on what we think is a crucial piece in the puzzle explaining the institutionalisation of policy instruments in the European Union.

Understanding the Power of Words through Discourse, Floating Signifiers and Storylines

Discourse analysis and discourse theory have infused research in EU studies, developing a growing literature mobilising the notion of 'discourse' or the label 'discourse analysis' (See for instance Diez, 1999; Radaelli, 1999; Schmidt, 2008; Crespy, 2010). This development has been paralleled with an extension of the concept of discourse, which conveys a host of different meanings according to scholars and studies. While mainstream trends have drawn on communication and argumentation theory and have taken discourse as one variable among others, this article adopts a different conception of discourse. Drawing from the work of Foucault, de Saussure and Laclau and Mouffe, it considers discourse as an ensemble of linguistic (and non-linguistic[2]) discursive practices that not only impact on interests and institutions but actually construct our overall understanding of reality. Hence, contrarily to predominant trends in European Studies, we do not conceive of discourse as 'a set of signs (of signifying elements *reflecting contents or representation*) but as practices which systematically *form the objects* which are talked about' (Foucault, 1969, p. 71; our emphases). As de Saussure explains, words do not entail concepts before the articulation of language, but are *empty* in essence (Saussure 1995). It is only through linguistic and non-linguistic discursive articulations between *signifiers* (the word – or: the sound-image) that words are actually given a meaning, i.e. bestowing a *signified* (the image linked to the word – or: the concept) (Saussure, 1995). What gives meaning to a signifier is its insertion in a *chain of equivalence and opposition* with other signifiers within a discourse (Saussure, 2002)[3]. To draw on an example given by Howarth, an object, e.g. a forest, might be articulated as an object of natural beauty, as an obstacle to the construction of a highway or as an ecosystem (Howarth, 2000, p. 10). The way the object is constructed depends upon the manner, in which it is linked to other signifiers such as aesthetics, urban development or ecology. Rather than merely influencing interests or institutions, discourse shapes and organises the way we see the world.

Furthermore, by articulating signifiers in certain ways, discourse not only shapes meaning but also performs the definition of what is commonly accepted as the right and only appropriate way of conceiving social reality. To follow up on Howarth's example, the specific articulation of the signifier 'tree' will change the very identity of the tree in our society, our identity towards the tree and what we see as right or wrong to do about the tree. Or to put it in Foucault's words, discourse determines a specific *regime of truth*, i.e., 'general politics of truth; that is the type of discourse which (a society) accepts and makes function as true' (Foucault, 1994, p. 158). Drawing on Laclau and Mouffe, we can consider that the imposition of a specific regime of truth occurs through two concomitant processes. On the one hand, this imposition takes place through the fixation of relations of identities in chains of equivalence such as 'a tree equals nature, which is equivalent to an object to be protected'. On the other, discourse consists in exclusionary practices, excluding other articulations from the legitimate common sense. Hence, if at a certain point, a dominant discourse predominantly articulates the tree as the object of environmental protection, the other representations of the tree will be disqualified and excluded from the system of meaning. By articulating a dominant vision of what is and what is not the right way of understanding the world, by articulating new identities and our common sense, discourse hence plays an essential role in relation to political action and power, which goes beyond sheer influence: it creates the space for possible and legitimate options; it defines what/who is and what/who is not considered as being legitimate and authorised, and what/who is to be excluded (Milliken, 1999).

To concretely understand the structuration of a dominant discourse, Laclau and Mouffe outline the importance of *nodal points*. Nodal points are privileged signifiers that partially fix the sense, binding together a particular system of meaning (Laclau & Mouffe, 2001, p. 112; Howarth & Stavrakis, 2000). This structuring and binding function is made possible because nodal points are also floating signifiers. The notion of floating signifier developed by Laclau refers to the unfixity of the relation between the signifier and the signified. It is when 'a plurality of signifieds is joined in an unstable fashion to certain signifiers, (and) that this instability does not depend entirely on the equivocality (the polysemous character) of the signifier but on the contexts in which the signifier is used' (Laclau, 1989, p. 70). To take Laclau's example, the signifier *democracy* used in the context of the cold war was floating for it was simultaneously present but articulated differently both in the communist and anti-communist discourses. Put differently, a floating signifier is 'a signifier that is overflowed with meaning because it is articulated differently within different discourses'

(Torfing, 1999, p. 301) competing or interacting with each other in the same argumentative context.

In this contribution, we add another level of analysis to this understanding of discourse domination through nodal points binding different systems of meaning and we combine this latter approach with Hajer's conception of discourse structuration through storylines (Hajer, 1995). Hajer argues that a discourse will structure (i.e., dominate the way a certain issue is interpreted) and be institutionalised (i.e., be consolidated in an institutional arrangement) thanks to the formation of a dominant discourse coalition encompassing different speakers, 'who, despite their different conceptions, are held together by a unique storyline' (Hajer, 2006, p. 65). Storylines are 'condensed statement summarising complex narratives, used by people as 'short hand' in discussions' (Hajer, 2006, p. 69) to make sense of a political issue, such as 'acid rains explain the death of trees' (Hajer, 1995). As Hajer put it, political actors will tend to use a specific storyline *assuming the hearer will know what he/she means*' (emphasis in original, Hajer, 2006, p. 302). Because storylines are short statements, they permit to bind different speakers and policy narratives together precisely because different interpretations of what is meant are possible. In this sense, storylines act in a similar way to nodal points that are floating signifiers. At the same time, a storyline may itself include a floating signifier, hence making the storyline even more ambiguous and potentially powerful. We will show that this is the case of the unfair trade storyline articulated in the European Parliament.

At the empirical level, the identification of nodal points, floating signifiers, storylines and discourse coalitions may help understand the imposition of a certain discourse to the expense of others, or understand its persistence. It can help understand how, at a given moment, one specific articulation of categories will impose its symbolic domination around a nodal point, and become a *regime of truth* delimiting the possibilities of speaking and acting, enabling and constraining the action of actors. In turn it permits to better illuminate the reasons of the institutionalisation of policy instruments, their preservation or disappearance. In this contribution, we draw on these conceptual tools to analyse the structuration of a discourse on unfair trade in the European Parliament. We argue that different MEPs are bound together around an unfair trade storyline, which has been made possible thanks to the floating status of the signifier 'unfair trade'. We will then show how unfair trade plays the role of a nodal point – a signifier that '"binds" or "orders" the other signifiers… in a way that unites and sediments a number of discourses' (Tregidga et al., 2011, p. 12).

The following section studies the storyline articulating *unfair trade*, while the next one highlights the multiple meanings given to unfair trade through the study of the chains of equivalence that are present within the European Parliament. Both parts are based on a survey of the debates related to trade remedies held during the current legislature. The debates selected address issues of 'unfair trade', 'trade defence instruments', or 'anti-dumping'. These debates encompass discussions within the International Trade Committee (INTR) (which are mainly 'questions and answers' with the European Commission) and discussions held in plenary sessions (which are mainly justifications of votes by MEPs).[4]

The Dominant Storyline in the European Parliament

In this part, we show that a specific storyline on unfair trade exists, shared by most MEPs and cutting across ideological cleavages. The methodology used to determine the existence and the content of this storyline is based on a search of the content (available online) of all the minutes of parliamentary debates and explanations of vote (hereafter: 'debates') from the current legislative session[5]. The material collected was then completed with a search of parliamentary reports. The search was first based on a search of the entry 'unfair trade'. The results were then narrowed down by limiting the results which appeared in the context of trade defence instruments in general or anti-dumping in particular. This context has been defined according to the matter discussed by parliamentarians but also by the content of the discussion itself. Hence, only debates that linked unfair trade with trade defence instruments were included.[6] It implies that debates discussing unfair trade from the unique point of view of fairness for producers (fair trade as understood by the fair trade labels) were not included. The selection process cannot be understood as a random search of all entries containing the expression 'unfair trade' but rather as an integral part of the interpretative method used in the article.

The interpretative methodology allows shedding light on one dominant storyline. This storyline is articulated around the notion of unfair trade, which appeared to be central in debates about anti-dumping and, more broadly, about the so-called 'trade defence instruments'. This storyline distinguishes between two kinds of 'trades' and prescribes what must be done against the unfair kind. The fight against unfair trade and the support for trade remedies is deeply ingrained within the European Parliament. This centrality is notably hammered by the Chair of the Committee on International Trade, MEP Vital Moreira:

> ... 'trade defence instruments', or anti-dumping and anti-subsidy measures... are essential to fair trade, as they constitute action that can be taken against unfair and anti-competitive trade practices by certain countries – China, for one – that cause serious harm to European companies within the European market itself. (Vital Moreira (S&D), European Parliament, 2011d)

Unfair trade is seen as harmful, which calls for fighting it and protecting the European market. The need of protection against unfair trade is also exemplified in the following statement: 'in matters concerning definitive anti-dumping measures, (it) is to be welcomed that we are establishing mechanisms which can protect the European market and which can protect our consumers' (Michał Tomasz Kamiński (ECR), European Parliament, 2012b).

In this context, two expressions using the notions of free and of fair trade have started to emerge in discourse about trade remedies: 'free *and* fair trade' and 'free *but* fair trade'. These expressions are nearly symmetrical, but not identical. The former expression is the official one adopted by the basic treaties of the European Union. The expression 'free and fair trade' was actually introduced recently, through the *Treaty of Lisbon amending the Treaty on European Union*. Article 3.5 of the consolidated version of the *Treaty on European Union* states that '[the Union] shall contribute to... free and fair trade'. The exact wording of Article 3.5 comes from Article I-3.4 (under the title 'The Union's objectives') of the stillborn *Treaty Establishing a Constitution for Europe*. In debates, it is noteworthy that this expression – 'free and fair' – is often used by those who praise the benefits of trade liberalisation in their argumentation:

> ... the existence of open and fair trade is a powerful tool for generating more growth and social welfare, building on the comparative advantages of each respective

economy and potential synergies flowing from greater economic integration and new inputs to a knowledge-driven economy. (Maria do Céu Patrão Neves (PPE), European Parliament, 2011a)

The latter expression – 'free but fair' – introduces a nuance and has developed in the context of the so-called 'trade defence instruments'. The conjunction 'but' parallels the need for defence in international trade. The use of the expression in this specific form has become widespread in talks about trade remedies, from the President of the European Commission ('We are in favour of free trade, as you know, but we are also in favour of fair trade'; José Manuel Barroso, President of the Commission, European Parliament, 2010e) to resolutions from the European Parliament ('ensure, within a balanced overall outcome, greater – *but fair* – competition'; European Parliament, Vital Moreira on behalf of the Committee on International Trade, 2011b).

If free trade is to be endorsed but, at the same time, if unfair trade is harmful, the issue (in the storyline) becomes about striking the right balance, hence 'the need to establish balanced trade' (Tokia Saïfi (PPE), 2012d). 'The European Union', adds this MEP, 'must first of all find a happy medium between ultra-free trade and protectionism... this third way must be embodied by the creation of a fair trade framework' (Tokia Saïfi (PPE), European Parliament, 2012d).

In brief, protectionism is noxious for the economy but 'unfair trade practices' or 'unfair competition' are equally damaging (See also Jacek Włosowicz (EFD), European Parliament, 2012c). Hence the need for a balanced trade policy. This understanding of the fight against unfair trade as both necessary but dangerous if conducted in an unmannered way is common in many discourses. 'Anti-dumping is a good servant but a bad master', says MEP Jan Zahradil:

> Just as it serves to protect European companies and the European economy from unfair competition and unfair commercial practices, so can it be abused in the interests of protectionism, unfortunately, to close European markets to imports from third countries. (Jan Zahradil, on behalf of the ECR Group – (CS), European Parliament, 2010b)

This articulation of the balance is also present among MEPs defining themselves as free-traders, such as MEP Robert Sturdy: 'While I agree that anti-dumping measures must be used where they are necessary, the problem is, of course, whether you use them as a protectionist measure' (Robert Sturdy, European Parliament, 2010b). More surprisingly, this articulation is also present among the fiercest proponents of trade remedies (see for instance: Niccolò Rinaldi (IT), European Parliament, 2010b).

Rare are the MEPs questioning this notion of 'unfair trade' or simply applying the standard of 'fair trade' as hereinabove described to the European Union herself. An increase in the use of trade remedies by the European Union is seen by many as 'a sign of the increase in unfair practices operated by other countries against European businesses' (Mario Pirillo, on behalf of the S&D Group – (IT), European Parliament, 2010b).

This exception notwithstanding, a broad convergence exists within the European Parliament around the discursive articulation we have described. The quotes selected above are indeed taken as examples and merely instantiate a broadly shared discourse on unfair trade. In this storyline, *unfair trade is harmful and must be distinguished from free and fair trade;*

there is a need to fight unfair trade with the help of the 'the trade defence instruments' (hence, the non-verbal metaphor of the shield on the website of the European Commission); *and there is therefore a need to strike the right balance in order to have 'free but free trade'*.

This storyline is clearly the dominant understanding of international economic relations within the European Parliament; and it is quasi-unanimously shared among speaking actors. But if a very broad consensus reigns about this storyline, the unpacking of the chains of equivalence (and opposition) in presence shows that MEPs link very different signifiers to the nodal point 'unfair trade'. Questions such as – *What is unfair trade? What kind of practices does it include? What practices should therefore be fought? To whom is it harmful?* – are answered in utterly different ways. As we show bellow, the kaleidoscopic reality behind 'unfair trade' implies that it is a floating signifier. Actors use different chains of equivalence around the nodal point *unfair trade* but the floating character of the node implies that they are nonetheless able to agree on the storyline we have just described.

Unfair Trade as a Floating Signifier

The theoretical part has posited that words find their meaning in connection with other signifiers. Looking at the signifier 'unfair trade' reveals that numerous chains of equivalence are connected to the nodal point *unfair trade*. This feature is particularly surprising given the consensus on the storyline we have just described. We therefore propose to highlight the main chains of equivalence in presence, and examine the conclusions that can be drawn from the character of unfair trade as a floating signifier. These different signifiers connected to unfair trade revolve around the issues of market economy, subsidies, competition, reciprocity, and social and environmental standards. To some extent, the presence of utterly different signifiers is logical, for trade defence instruments are meant to fight different realities defined by law. These are dumping – as defined by European and WTO law – and subsidies. Anti-dumping law also provides for the application of a special (less favourable) treatment of so-called non-market economies. What debates show, however, is that the boundaries are not as clear-cut within the discourse of political actors as these legal definitions. Political actors use definitions different from the law; they stick to one understanding; or they use expandable definitions of the practice regarded as 'unfair'. Hence, the use of the notion of floating signifier permits to shed light on the 'kaleidoscopic' discursive construction of unfair trade.

Unfair Trade as Trade with Non-market Economies

The chain articulating the 'market economy' with unfair trade and the corollary differential treatment applied to non-market economies find their origin in the Cold War (Snyder, 2001; Horne, 2006). The label 'non-market economy' was created in a specific context, but it has remained deeply ingrained in spite of massive changes. In the chain of equivalence, 'unfair trade' stems from having economic relations with non-market economies, which are defined as economies that do not play by the rules of the market. This discursive connection is notably used by MEP Christine De Veyrac (PPE):

> ... this will allow fighting against unfair competition from some foreign companies. Dealers who import from countries that do not respect the rules of the market

economy will have to pay higher tariffs on the borders of Europe. It is indeed necessary to protect our businesses against this distorted competition that we can no longer tolerate! (Christine De Veyrac (PPE), European Parliament, 2012c; our translation)

Another chain of equivalence, which is *de facto* close to the chain articulating non-market economies, refers to unfair trade as resulting from states' subsidies. This connection is particularly explicit in the following excerpt from MEP Daniel Caspary, who links both distortions of competition and illegitimate advantage to state subsidies: 'We must be able to defend ourselves if other countries distort competition using state subsidies' (Daniel Caspary (DE), 2010b). Taking the example of a non-market economy – China – MEP Henri Weber explains that 'Chinese exporting companies receive massive aid from state banks and local authorities', concluding that 'Our European industries are under threat in the light of such unfair competition' (Henri Weber (S&D), 2010a). Mirroring the criticism of non-market economies, state subsidies also equate government intervention in the economy. In the case of China, MEP Hans-Peter Martin points to the Chinese renewable energy industry where China 'acts massively in order to secure a technological edge to their own industry' (Hans-Peter Martin (NI), European Parliament, 2012d).

The criticism directed at state intervention often goes hand in hand with a call for positive action. Finding 'ways of reciprocity and conditions of fair competition' (Marielle de Sarnez (ALDE), European Parliament, 2012d) is therefore not limited to fighting these practices through trade remedies in order to defend the European economy. Marielle de Sarnez, rapporteur for the report *EU and China: unbalanced trade?*, commands not only to develop 'a European strategy, particularly in terms of production, in terms of re-industrialization, research and innovation', but also to launch an 'offensive strategy', which may imply the need to 'preserve sometimes entire sectors for economic development' (Marielle de Sarnez, European Parliament, 2012d). This kind of call for a comprehensive industrial policy is widespread and is articulated with the *metaphor of the balance* from the *unfair trade storyline*. MEP Kader Arif urges to design: 'a new strategy that strikes the right balance between openness, protection and support', adding that:

> ... when we are faced with unfair practices, it is clear that protection is necessary, but the principle of it must be accepted and defended internationally and the sometimes false accusations of protectionism (must be) dismissed once and for all. (Kader Arif, on behalf of the S&D Group, European Parliament, 2012d)

Not only this excerpt sticks to the implicit of the storyline that unfair trade practices are present in other players' actions, not in European's, but the issue of what should be done about unfair trade brings a new interesting element. Indeed, the call for European economic intervention in response to similar intervention by other states raises the issue of the role of the state in the economy. It is therefore surprising that this issue is not a bone of contention in debates on unfair trade, for positions on state intervention are supposedly radically different among the political streams in presence. It may imply that, if unfair trade was discursively unpacked, dissensions would most probably appear.

Unfair Trade as a Distortion of Competition

A different chain of equivalence directly links unfair trade to the register of competition policy. However paradoxical, as trade remedies do not include competition criteria and can even contribute to create or sustain monopolies, this chain is the main line of justification of 'trade defence instruments' within the European Commission. In the absence of international rules on competition (and the burial of the so-called Singapore issues at the World Trade Organization, which included negotiations on competition rules), the European Commission argues that trade remedies – or 'trade defence instruments' – are the only tools available to fight 'distortions of competition'. This discursive articulation is exemplified by Commissioner De Gucht's answer to the European Parliament:

> I am happy that the European Parliament shares our view that the defence of EU production against international trade distortions should be considered as a necessary component of an open and fair trade strategy... Now, continuing on the broader issues, trade defence instruments are there for good reasons. In the absence of international competition rules and other rules associated with properly functioning markets, trade defence instruments are the only possible means of protecting our industry against unfairly traded goods. (Karel De Gucht, European Commissioner for Trade, European Parliament, 2010c)

The chain of equivalence linking unfair trade to 'distortion of competition' is also common within the European Parliament. Here, unfair trade practices are worded in the vocabulary of competition and equated to a form of 'distortion of competition'. This is exemplified by MEP Carlo Fidanza (PPE): 'it is necessary to deal with problems related to market distortions (by) ensuring consistency of business behaviours to international rules on free competition' (Carlo Fidanza (PPE), European Parliament, 2012c).

This connection with competition is present in a number of expressions, which all seem to point to the same issue: 'protecting European businesses against anti-competitive practices' (Sergio Paolo Francesco Silvestris (PPE), European Parliament, 2012b); the existence of alteration in 'the nature of the markets' or the 'market conditions' (Giovanni La Via (PPE), European Parliament, 2012c); or 'serious distortion of competition' (Nuno Melo (PPE), European Parliament, 2012c). In these variations, the notion of distortion is used to equate to the notion of dumping, which seems to become itself a new floating signifier (see for instance Elisabeth Köstinger (PPE), 2012c).

This understanding of unfair trade as distortion of competition – often condensed in the expression 'unfair competition' – has become highly common within the European Parliament, and thus adopts or parallels the chain of equivalence put forward by the European Commission (*unfair trade as distortions of competition*). For many MEPs, unfair trade and unfair competition are not only equivalent but they are purely and simply synonyms.

Unfair Trade as Social Dumping

The most common, and perhaps the most complex, chain of equivalence mobilises the notion of social dumping – in conjunction with the notion of environmental dumping – in relation to the node unfair trade. Unfair trade equates, for this coalition, lax or inexistent standards in matters of social rights and environmental protection. Unfair trade arises, in the words of MEP Fiorello Provera, from countries 'in which the protection of social and environmental rights is in fact non-existent' (Fiorello Provera (EFD), European Parliament, 2012c). Even if they are sometimes mentioned together, we will discuss the specific issue of social dumping in this subsection, while the expanding issue of environmental dumping will be analysed in a subsection of its own.

The understanding of unfair trade as social dumping further increase the ambiguity over the meaning of unfair trade. Unfair trade is due to lax (or inexistent) social standards but also to sheer differences in the cost of labour, which implies a call for equality of conditions:

> ... cheap labour and social dumping are methods which are used very frequently in developing and emerging countries. The problem of anti-dumping shows how important it is to call for environmental and social standards, in particular, and also trade protection measures during negotiations on free trade agreements with third countries. (Elisabeth Köstinger (PPE) – (DE), European Parliament, Wednesday, 2010b)

The issue of equality of condition is an old one. In the case of the United States, Beviglia Zampeti (2006) explains that preoccupations over equality of conditions thought as an issue of fairness were present at the very beginning of discussions on American trade policy. This is the same understanding of fairness that would drive the proponents of the famous Hawley-Smoot Tariff Act, which increased US tariffs after the Great Depression (Beviglia Zampeti, 2006, pp. 51–66).

In the European Parliament, this chain of equivalence articulates unfair trade as harmful both for Europeans and for people in the exporting countries. Fighting unfair trade is thus good for Europeans and good for third countries (Françoise Castex (S&D), European Parliament, 2011a). In this perspective, fighting the damaging effects of unfair trade helps prevent harm for Europeans but also helps improve the dire conditions of people around the world. The defence against unfair trade is thus doubly beneficial (see also on multinationals 'using slaves or underpaid farm workers': Lorenzo Fontana, rapporteur for the opinion of the Committee on Agriculture and Rural Development, European Parliament, 2012a).

The debates on the *Report on human rights and social and environmental standards in international trade agreements* (European Parliament, 2010g) also connects the conditions of production (and lax standards) with the intrinsic dangerousness of the products, where unfair trade results from the ability of foreign producers of 'using cheap materials and not paying attention to workmanship', making possible 'to achieve low retail prices and to flood markets' (Jarosław Kalinowski (PPE), European Parliament, 2010b). This perspective leads to calls for stringent control over process and production methods (PPMs) in order to 'guarantee that all our businesses have fair conditions of competition' (Jarosław Kalinowski (PPE), 2010b). The standards that have to be respected, however, are not precisely circumscribed and they often equates to European standards:

> [European] businesses have to comply with extremely demanding standards of worker protection, meet high wages and tax bills, abide by laws placing strict controls on emissions into the environment, and abide by conditions imposed by local planning regulations. (Oreste Rossi (EFD), European Parliament, 2010d)

Similarly, trade with Latin America poses the same kind of problem to many MEPs: 'Mercosur products are not required to meet the same environmental and social standards as their European counterparts – conditions under which there is a real risk of unfair competition' (Christine De Veyrac (PPE), European Parliament, 2011a). Competing with foreign businesses which are 'obviously not subject to such controls and rules' (idem) is therefore unfair.

This notion of absolute advantage is itself articulated as an 'unfair competitive advantage', as coined by the rapporteur of the *Report on human rights and social and environmental standards in international trade agreements* (European Parliament, 2010g): the solution is to 'require imported goods to comply with the same social and environmental standards as European products... If this is not done, the unfair competitive advantage will mean that the EU is no longer able to compete with low cost and low quality imports' (Marielle De Sarnez (ALDE), European Parliament, 2010d). The same MEP stated that:

> ... the ridiculously low labour costs and despicable working conditions should no longer be seen by the Commission as 'natural competitive advantages'. On this point, Commissioner, I insist that the Commission changes its doctrine. (Marielle De Sarnez (ALDE), European Parliament, 21 September 2010)

This chain of equivalence is therefore often articulated with the need of *reciprocity* in international trade ('Europe's approach is based on reciprocity' (Elisabeth Köstinger (PPE), European Parliament, 22 May 2012)). The basic idea behind reciprocity is that the same level of concessions must be offered so as to ensure fair trade: 'we need reciprocity. For example, Chinese companies cannot continue setting up shops in Europe when European companies are denied access to their public market' (Marielle De Sarnez (ALDE), European Parliament, 21 September 2010). If Europe is open, the same must be true of trade partners:

> China must not be allowed to shut off the Chinese market to foreign companies. Mr De Gucht, in committee, you said to us that the European Union should be 'open, but not naively open'. I very much share your view... Please make sure that you speak in this way in China. (Daniel Caspary (PPE), European Parliament, 2010a)

But reciprocity is not solely connected to issues of market access, it is also about the respect of the same standards and the respect of the rules of international trade laws: 'if the European Union complies with binding standards, it must also be able to require the same from its trading partners and particularly from emerging countries' (Vilija Blinkevičiūtė (S&D), European Parliament, 2010d). It is therefore necessary that these standards apply 'to all the players' (Cristiana Muscardini (PPE), European Parliament, 2012b). In this perspective the application of European standards transforms the European trade policy into 'an instrument in the service of the European Union's overall objectives', where:

> ... trade is seen not as an end in itself, but rather as a tool for the promotion of European commercial interests, and as an instrument for fair trade that can bring into general practice the effective inclusion and implementation of social and environmental standards with all EU trade partners. (José Manuel Fernandes (PPE), European Parliament, 2010d)

With regard to the coexistence or struggle of multiple chains of equivalence connected to the nodal point *unfair trade*, it is noteworthy that some MEPs criticise the notion of reciprocity for being 'an incredibly emotive word that means very different things to people' and 'one should be careful about using the word reciprocity' (Morten Løkkegaard, European Parliament, 2012d). MEP Daniel Caspary adds that he calls for replacing this notion by notions such as 'fair competition' or 'so-called level playing field' (Daniel Caspary (PPE), European Parliament, 2012d), which is actually the language used by the European Commission. These two comments manifestly show that MEPs are sometimes self-conscious of the power of words.

Unfair Trade as Environmental Dumping

The elasticity of some chains of equivalence is particularly obvious in the case of environmental dumping. The discursive articulations present in this chain resort to articulations used in other chains, leading to expansion rather than confrontation:

> ... it is also important not only to safeguard the interests of producers, but also to include the interests of consumers... namely to put a stop to dumping below actual costs... the actual costs must include environmental dumping. Obtaining an economic advantage by circumventing environmental legislation is just like obtaining another form of subsidy besides economic dumping, but in the form of the environment. (Carl Schlyter (SV), European Parliament, 2010b)

This chain of equivalence integrating environmental concerns also includes calls for reviewing the definition of provisions related to trade remedies in WTO law as including environmental dumping (European Parliament, 2010f). This articulation of environmental dumping has led to the willingness 'to refer cases of social or environmental dumping to either the ILO or a World Environmental Organisation, which needs to be created with all possible speed' (Marielle De Sarnez (ALDE), European Parliament, 2010d).

Rather than confronting trade liberalisation, this chain of equivalence implicitly endorses the metaphor of the balance from the *unfair trade* storylines, by considering that 'trade liberalisation can conflict with climate protection if certain countries seek a competitive advantage by failing to act on climate issues' (European Parliament, 2010f). The concrete effects of this articulation of environmental dumping to the nodal point *unfair trade* are mitigated. On the one hand, most MEPs advocating for the expansion of dumping to environmental issues seem unsatisfied by the meagre progress made by the European Commission on this issue. On the other hand, the expansion perfectly sticks to the *unfair trade* storylines and the European Commission seems to have no solution but to endorse it:

> ... if a company were to raise the issue that you put forward concerning carbon leakage, then the Commission would, of course, investigate and see whether the case ought to result in measures being imposed. But the issue is certainly not beyond the scope of the arguments that we consider. (De Gucht, European Parliament, 2010c)

In summary, the *unfair trade* storyline is articulated within a series of different chains of equivalence. The principal chains equate unfair trade to trade with non-market economies or economies that use state subsidies; to distortions of competition; to social dumping; and to environmental dumping. These chains of equivalence do not simply overlap the legal definitions of trade defence instruments (trade remedies); they expand their definitions (equating 'dumping' as trade with non-market economies, for instance). Accordingly, actors rallying around the notion of unfair trade do not share the same concerns. The existence of a floating signifier within the storyline, nonetheless, permits actors to rally albeit they do not share the same understanding of what unfair trade means.

Conclusion

The 'unfair trade' storyline is the dominant one in the European Parliament. This storyline equates unfair trade with a harmful practice and calls on striking the right balance in order to preserve free trade while fighting unfair trade practices. The direct corollary of this battle is the need to resort to 'trade defence instruments'. Given this articulation, little contestation has emerged within the Parliament about the rationale behind trade remedies, such as anti-dumping or countervailing duties. Either there is actually no opposition to this storyline, or this opposition is not expressed through explanation of votes, debates in commission, or parliamentary reports. Whatever the reasons, it must be deduced that a peculiar regime of truth reigns over unfair trade. The concrete effects are that this regime of truth masks the internal contradictions of trade remedies and the tensions underlying the use of trade remedies.

From a theoretical point of view, this analysis has permitted to demonstrate the relevance of a series of concepts developed by discourse analysis in order to shed light on the meaning given by actors to policy instruments. The combination of the notion of storyline proposed by Hajer with the notion of floating signifier allows outlining dimensions that might have remained in the shadow by simply looking at ideas or at the interactive utterance of ideas. The corollary, as we have shown, is that floating signifiers make consensus possible on issues that might seem *a priori* divisive. Explaining the discursive structuration and the deep institutionalisation of the discourse on trade remedies therefore requires to consider the key role played by the notion of 'unfair trade' and to look at its character as a floating signifier.

From a more practical standpoint, the article has dug into the power of words and the regime of truth in order to highlight the peculiar mechanisms at work. This task echoes the preoccupation of Lindsey and Ikenson (2003) with the rhetorical advantage enjoyed in the United States by proponents of the battle against unfair trade. According to these (libertarian) policy experts, the current terms of the debate 'strongly favour maintenance of the status quo' (Lindsey & Ikenson, 2003, pp. 150), adding that:

> Defenders of antidumping have been able to create and hold this rhetorical advantage because they have never been required to define 'fairness' and 'level playing field' or explain how current antidumping rules advance those admirable-sounding goals. They simply assert the connection between current antidumping rules and fairness…

This article has therefore permitted to unveil some of the discursive mechanisms at play, and in the case of the European Union, those mechanisms of what Lindsey and Ikenson call a 'rhetorical advantage'.

The results of our discursive analysis imply that the current process of 'modernisation' of the 'trade defence instruments' launched by the European Commission will suffer no attempt from members of the European Parliament to weaken these instruments, and will not even endure simply vague attempts to thoroughly assess the aim of trade remedies (or their justification), their actual targets and their actual result. While the European Commission has yet to come up with a more elaborated rationale for the use of 'trade defence instruments', little pressure will be felt from the European Parliament. Neither will we see any debate on the meaning of unfair trade practices. Perhaps, people will simply state that they recognise unfair trade when they see it.

In this context, a real debate on the different chains of equivalence in presence might be healthy. There may be a political case for trade remedies. The idea that globalisation and trade liberalisation must be managed is politically defensible. But the current, superficial, debate does little good. A reflection on trade remedies, in terms of the *de facto* monopolies and the high prices imposed upon consumers is much needed.

Finally, by calling attention to aspects that are *not* included in discourse, the analysis has also shown another important element for international economic governance. The usual articulation of the storyline indeed barely applies the criteria of unfair trade to the European Union itself. In this context, the growing resort to trade remedies by emerging countries can only be apprehended as some more unfair practices imposed on the European Union, while the question whether trade remedies are there for good reasons or not remains unanswered. Only a true debate on the different chains of equivalence linked to the nodal point *unfair trade* might give us some clues on the political and economic case for trade remedies.

Notes

[1] For a discussion of the methodological issues related to measuring the use of trade remedies, see Vandenbussche and Viegelahn (2011); see also Zanardi (2004).

[2] In this research, we mainly focus on linguistic practices but we acknowledge the importance of non-linguistic practices.

[3] On the difference between Saussure's structuralist understanding of discourse and Laclau and Mouffe's post-structuralist approach, see Philips and Jorgensen (2002).

[4] The 'debates' analysed in this article consist of both parliamentary debates and explanations of vote, i.e., oral or written statements in plenary sessions. It is therefore possible that the content of these statements can be in part regarded as 'political posturing', i.e., the expression of a political position that is deemed politically rewarding. These political statements may include the willingness to express sympathy for workers of the MEP's nationality affected by international competition, disagreement with the official stance of the MEP's home government, or any electoral consideration. In this article, however, we do not consider the motivation behind the construction of the discourse on trade defence instruments, but exclusively the construction of this discourse itself. We consider that, whatever the political motivations of actors, it is crucial, even from a policy view point, to understand how trade remedies are discursively constructed.

[5] Within the European Parliament, speaking time is allocated during plenary sessions according to the size of political groups (European Parliament, Rules of Procedure of the European Parliament – 7th parliamentary term – January 2013, Rule n° 149 [Allocation of speaking time and list of speakers]. Available at www.europarl.europa.eu/sides/getLastRules.do?language = EN&reference = TOC). Groups then in turn decide which members will receive speaking time. But the speakers are also selected according to a 'catch-the-eyes' principle; in this case, the President selects MEPs having indicating their willingness to speak during the debates. Furthermore, MEPs who would not have had the opportunity to speak have the possibility to include a statement of up to 200 words for inclusion in the verbatim. From the point of view of 'representativeness', the procedural rules imply that all political groups present in the European Parliament should have had the opportunity to express themselves. It is possible, however, that the MEPs

willing to speak through the speaking time allocated to political group or through the 'catch-the-eyes' principle and written statements are the most concerned by 'unfair trade' and trade defence instruments. Given the fact that we are not interested in the motivations of MEPs but rather in the dominant discourse, or regime of truth, present in the parliament, the issue is nonetheless not problematic.

[6] The debates include issues such as: general discussions on anti-dumping cases; questions with the President of the Commission; climate change; human rights and social and environmental standards in international trade agreements; exceptional trade measures for countries and territories participating in or linked to the European Union's Stabilisation and Association process; the Community regime for the control of exports, transfer, brokering and transit of dual use items; EU–Canada trade relations; a raw materials strategy for Europe; the state of play of the negotiations on the Doha Development Agenda; the Community regime for the control of exports of dual-use items and technology; the agreement between the EU and Morocco concerning reciprocal liberalisation measures on agricultural products and fishery products; a proposal for a regulation of the European Parliament and of the Council amending certain regulations relating to the common commercial policy as regards the procedures for the adoption of certain measures; restrictions on imports of certain steel products from Russia; protection against dumped imports from countries not members of the European Community; the report: EU and China – unbalanced trade?; the EU–China summits; measures to protect the EU market from unusually low priced imports of Chinese.

References

All European Parliament Minutes are Available at: http://www.europarl.europa.eu/plenary/en/home.html (European Parliament/Plenary); http://www.europarl.europa.eu/committees/en/home.html (European Parliament/Committees)

Beviglia Zampeti (2006) *Fairness in the World Economy. US Perspectives on International Trade Relations* (Cheltenham: Edward Elgar).

Cass, R. & Boltuk, R. (1997) Antidumping and countervailing-duty law: The mirage of equitable international competition, in: J. Bhagwati & R. Hudec (Eds) *Fair Trade and Harmonization: Legal analysis* (Vol. 2), pp. 351–414 (Cambridge: Massachusetts Institute of Technology).

Crespy, A. (2010) When 'Bolkestein' is trapped by the French anti-liberal discourse: a discursive-institutionalist account of preference formation in the realm of European Union multi-level politics, *Journal of European Public Policy*, 17(8), pp. 1253–1270.

Diez, T. (1999) Speaking 'Europe': The politics of integration discourse, *Journal of European Public Policy*, 6(4), pp. 598–613.

European Commission (2006) Communication global Europe. Competing in the world: A contribution to the EU's growth and jobs strategy. Available at http://trade.ec.europa.eu/doclib/docs/2006/october/tradoc_130376.pdf (accessed 22 October 2012).

European Commission (2011) Karel De Gucht, 'Trade – a growth engine in the crisis', speech given at The States General of Foreign Trade, Rome, 28 October 2011. Available at http://trade.ec.europa.eu/doclib/docs/2011/october/tradoc_148335.pdf (accessed 22 October 2012).

European Commission (2012a) Karel De Gucht, 'A trade defence system for today's global economy', speech at the *High Level Conference: Modernisation of Trade Defence Instruments*, Brussels, 10 May 2012. Available at http://trade.ec.europa.eu/doclib/docs/2012/may/tradoc_149424.pdf (accessed 22 October 2012).

European Commission (2012b) Factsheet, Why the EU's investigation into solar panel imports from China does not harm Europe's climate goals, Brussels, 10 September 2012. Available at http://trade.ec.europa.eu/doclib/docs/2012/september/tradoc_149903.pdf (accessed 22 October 2012).

European Parliament (2010a) Plenary debates, Point 4: EU–China summit on 6 October 2010, Tuesday, 21 September 2010, Strasbourg.

European Parliament (2010b) Debates, Point 21: Anti-dumping cases – state of play and prospects, CRE 24/11/2010-21 (O-0132/2010), Wednesday, 24 November 2010, Strasbourg (INTA).

European Parliament (2010c) Karel De Gucht, 'Speaking points: Anti-dumping cases state of play and perspectives', answer to oral questions, 24 November 2010, Strasbourg. Available at http://trade.ec.europa.eu/doclib/docs/2010/november/tradoc_147051.pdf (accessed 22 October 2012).

European Parliament (2010d) Plenary debates, Point 9: Explanations of votes, A7-0275/2010, Thursday, 25 November 2010, Strasbourg.

European Parliament (2010e) Plenary debates, question hour with the President of the Commission, Tuesday, 14 December 2010, Strasbourg.

European Parliament, Report (2010f) Report on international trade policy in the context of climate change imperatives (2010/2103(INI)), 'Making international trade prices fairer and avoiding carbon leakage', Committee on International Trade, A7-0310/2010, PE 448.802v02-00, 8 November 2010.

European Parliament, Report (2010g) 'Report on human rights and social and environmental standards in international trade agreements' (2009/2219(INI)), A7-0312/2010, PE 445.733v02-00, 8 November 2010.

European Parliament (2011a) Plenary debates, Point 6: Explanations of vote, CRE 11/05/2011–5.12 (A7-0243/2010), Wednesday, 11 May 2011, Strasbourg.

European Parliament (2011b) Motion for a resolution, resolution on EU–Canada trade relations further to question for oral answer B7, 0213/2011 pursuant to Rule 115(5) of the Rules of Procedure on EU–Canada trade relations (Document B7-0344/2011), PE465.635v01-00, 26 May 2011.

European Parliament (2011c) Plenary debates, explanations of votes, CRE 12/09/2011–20 (Document B7-0478/2011), Monday, 12 September 2011, Strasbourg.

European Parliament (2011d) Plenary debates, Point 9: Explanations of vote, CRE 04/04/2011–15, Tuesday, 27 September 2011, Strasbourg.

European Parliament (2012a) Plenary debates, 'Point 3: Agreement between the EU and Morocco concerning reciprocal liberalisation measures on agricultural products and fishery products (debate)', CRE 14/02/2012–13 (Document A7-0023/2012), Tuesday, 14 February 2012, Strasbourg.

European Parliament (2012b) Plenary debates, Point 10: Explanations of vote, PV 14/03/2012–9.1 (Document A7-0447/2011), Wednesday, 14 March 2012, Strasbourg.

European Parliament (2012c) Plenary debates, explanations of votes, PV 10/05/2012–12.1, Thursday, 10 May 2012, Brussels.

European Parliament (2012d) Plenary debates, explanations of votes, Point 13: EU and China: Unbalanced trade?, CRE 22/05/2012–13 (Document A7-0141/2012), Tuesday, 22 May 2012, Strasbourg.

Foucault, M. (1969) *L'archéologie du savoir* (Paris: Gallimard).

Foucault, M. (1994/1977) *Dits et écrits* (Paris: Gallimard).

Hajer, M. (1995) *The Politics of Environmental Discourse. Ecological Modernization and the Policy Process* (Oxford: Oxford University Press).

Hajer, M. (2006) Doing discourse analysis: Coalitions, practices, meaning, in: M. Van den Brink & T. Metze (Eds) *Words Matter in Policy and Planning. Discourse Theory and Method in the Social Sciences*, pp. 65–74 (Utrecht: Netherland Geographical Studies).

Hoekman, B. & Kostecki, M. (2001) *The Political Economy of the World Trading System. The WTO and Beyond* (2nd ed.) (Oxford: Oxford University Press).

Horne, C. (2006) *Post-Communist Economies and Western Trade Discrimination* (Basingstoke: Palgrave Macmillan).

Howarth, D. (2000) *Discourse* (New York: Open University Press).

Laclau, E. (1989) Politics and the limits of modernity, *Social Text*, No. 21, pp. 63–82.

Laclau, E. (1996) Why do empty signifiers matter to politics?, in: E. Laclau (Ed.) *Emancipation(S)*, pp. 36–46 (London: Verso).

Laclau, E. & Mouffe, C. (2001) *Hegemony and Socialist Strategy: Towards a Radical Democratic Politics* (London and New York: Verso).

Lindsey, B. & Ikenson, D. (2003) *Antidumping Exposed. The Devilish Details of Unfair Trade Law* (Washington, DC: Cato Institute).

Lowenfeld, A. (2008) *International Economic Law* (Oxford: Oxford University Press).

Mavroidis, P., Messerlin, P. & Wauters J. (2008) *The Law and Economics of Contingent Protection in the WTO* (Cheltenham: Edward Elgar Publishing).

Methmann, C. P. (2010) 'Climate protection' as empty signifier: A discourse theoretical perspective on climate mainstreaming in world politics, *Millenium–Journal of International Studies*, 39(2), pp. 345–372.

Milliken, J. (1999) The study of discourse in international relations: A critique of research and methods, *European Journal of International Relations*, 5(2), pp. 225–244.

Phillips, L. & Jorgensen, M. W. (2002) *Discourse Analysis as Theory and Method* (London: Sage).

Radaelli, C. (1999) Harmful tax competition in the EU: Policy narratives and advocacy coalitions, *Journal of Common Market Studies*, 37(4), pp. 661–682.

Saussure, F. (1995/1916) *Cours de linguistique générale* (Paris: Payot).

Saussure, F. (2002) *Ecrits de linguistique générale* (Paris: Gallimard).

Schmidt, V. A. (2008) Discursive institutionalism: The Explanatory power of ideas and discourse, *Annual Review of Political Science*, 11(1), pp. 303–326.

Snyder, F. (2001) The origins of the 'nonmarket economy': Ideas, pluralism and power in EC anti-dumping law about China, *European Law Journal*, 7(4), pp. 369–424.

Torfing, J. (1999) *New Theories of Discourse: Laclau, Mouffe and Zizek* (Oxford: Blackwell).

Tregidga, H. M., Milne, M. J. & Kearins, K. N. (2010) *Sustainable Development as a Floating Signifier: The Foundations for Resistance and Change in the Organisational Context*. Paper presented at the Journal of Management Studies Conference, Loughborough University, UK 27-29 September 2010.

Vandenbussche, H. & Viegelahn C. (2011) European Union: No protectionist surprises, in: C.P., Bown (Ed.) *The Great Recession and Import Protection. The Role of Temporary Trade Barriers* (Washington, DC: The World Bank). pp. 85–130.

WTO (2012) Statistics on anti-dumping, anti-dumping initiations: By reporting member 01/01/1995–31/12/2011. Available at http://www.wto.org/english/tratop_e/adp_e/AD_InitiationsByRepMem.pdf (accessed 22 October 2012).

Zanardi, M. (2004) Anti-dumping: What are the numbers to discuss at Doha?, *The World Economy*, 27(3), pp. 403–433.

'Bursting the Brussels Bubble': Using Ethnography to Explore the European Parliament as a Transnational Political Field

AMY BUSBY
Sussex European Institute, University of Sussex, UK

ABSTRACT   *This article explores what ethnography can tell us about the practice of politics inside the European Parliament (EP). It responds to calls from within the discipline for a more sociological approach to the EU institutions and research which makes the real world of politics visible. The paper argues that an ethnographic methodology coupled with a Bourdieusian theoretical framework enables deeper exploration of the everyday practice of politics by individual MEPs and therefore a more nuanced understanding of political behaviour within this institutional context. First, it identifies the gap to which it hopes to contribute, discusses the growing sociological literature of the EU, and introduces ethnography. Then it discusses Bourdieu's structural constructivism and outlines relevant thinking tools, with particular reference to Adler-Nissen's work. The paper then applies the theoretical framework to data gathered through ethnographic fieldwork and elite interviews, aiming to open up the black-box and illuminate practices occurring inside. The EP is conceptualised as a transnational political field with a system of positions and power relations, where doxa operates beneath a habitus of dispositions, and where actors employ their position and capital in strategies to influence what is at stake in the game.*

Our understanding of EU politics – as it is conventionally described – is mostly limited to the picture created by political scientists, economists, and legal scholars. In this picture, the EU is either a depersonalised, self-sustaining institutional complex, or… a battleground of super-individuals… What is missing from our understanding of the EU is a human dimension. A sociological account makes clear what should be self-evident: the EU does not do anything by itself; it is people as everyday political agents who make the EU happen. (Kauppi, 2011, p. 150)

The European integration process is largely a socially driven process. To understand it, one must therefore explore its social character. (Adler-Nissen, 2009, p. 15)

'Bursting the Brussels Bubble': An Ethnographic Approach

In Spring 2010, I began my search for a place to live during fieldwork in Brussels; an essential task for any ethnographer you won't find routinely mentioned in *How To Do A PhD* guides. Asking Brussels-based friends for advice, most recommended I stay in the European Quarter; convenient and where most interns live, although probably a little pricey, a bit soulless, and dead at the weekend. I ended up living on rue Wiertz, with a view of the European Parliament (EP) from my window, and thereafter spent seven months living deep inside the 'Brussels bubble'. I soon heard this ubiquitous phrase used by the staff of the EP and other Brussels-based organisations as they gathered on Place Lux, the bar-laden square in front of the EP where people often meet on Thursday and Friday evenings to discuss the week, as well as in interviews. The 'Brussels bubble' refers to the peculiarities of working in Brussels; a multinational and multilingual space, an intense environment with a distinct rhythm to life, where people come and go continuously but which feels like a small village where everyone seems to know each other and news travels fast.

This pervasive and taken-for-granted metaphor indicates a starting point for a sociological analysis of the EP. This institutional context can be conceptualised as a transnational political field with a particular elite habitus, and this approach can help us understand individuals' behaviour within it. Adler-Nissen takes a sociological approach to the Council and uses an inspiring theoretical framework which reminds us that it is people who conduct European processes (2009, p. 22). Bourdieu's framework, from a scholar who tried to understand the relationship between peoples' practices and their context (Webb et al., 2002, p. 21), is one within which we can situate the behaviour of actors to help gain a deeper understanding of the practice of politics inside the EP. Conceptualising the EP as a transnational political field with a particular habitus, where capital is accumulated and strategies employed, can help us gain a more nuanced understanding of political behaviour. Coupled with ethnography, it enables deeper exploration of the institutional context, meanings actors attribute to it, and behaviour within it. This paper takes this methodological approach to the EP to deepen our understanding of the everyday practice of politics by individual MEPs within this context, contributing to a growing sociology of the EU institutions and the nascent body of anthropological work on the EU. Like all the perspectives presented in this special issue, ethnography can challenge the mainstream in EU studies, particularly the approach taken to institutions, because it highlights the role of agency and agents and how they negotiate structures – or the particular historical and social moments in which they find themselves (Forsey, 2004, p. 69, Rosen, 1991, p. 12) – and construct reality. Like discourse theory and analysis, ethnography is at an early stage in EU studies (Demossier, 2011; Bourne & Cini, 2005, p. 6) and also is not a general theory of European integration but instead can illuminate certain aspects of European integration processes and politics. As Hilmer notes: 'the goal of political scientists who seek to promote more ethnography in their discipline is to contribute, rather than radically transform' (2011, p. 100).

The EP is an institution which has seen its powers gradually and continuously enhanced with each EU treaty and has seen academic interest intensify accordingly; writing being 'a function of its powers and prestige' (Hix et al., 2003, p. 192). The first generation of MEP (voting) behaviour research was quantitative and analysed plenary roll call votes (RCVs). Broadly it found that the EP groups have become increasingly cohesive, the group and national party delegation the best predictors of votes, and that despite high heterogeneity

EP politics has become increasingly structured. Recent RCV analysis has also led to the rejection of the functionalist assumption that MEPs *go native* in Brussels as voting behaviour does not become more pro-EU (Scully, 2005). This research generation urges scholars to approach the EP as a *normal* parliament rather than a *sui generis* institution (Hix et al., 2007; Yordanova, 2011, Bale & Taggart, 2006; McElroy, 2006, p. 179). Whilst it has significantly contributed to explaining outcomes, it has left us knowing 'surprisingly little' about internal pre-plenary processes (Ringe, 2010), roles of actors, and the everyday practice of politics.

Despite growing quantities of research, our understanding of EP legislative politics has remained in its 'infancy' (McElroy, 2006, p. 176). Like Jenson and Mérand, I argue this is partly due to the under-socialised nature of the literature which is 'dominated by a narrow form of institutionalism' (2010, p. 74). They recommend a return to the sociological roots of neo-institutionalism, where researchers don't need to 're-invent the wheel' as it is grounded in the legacy of scholars such as Weber and Durkheim from where inspiration can be drawn (2010, pp. 74–76). Kauppi says that even social constructivism, 'despite its stated aims to study the social fabric of European and world politics, it is only weakly sociological' (2003, p. 777). He finds a theory of agency is still absent because political action is not situated in specific institutional settings, and social constructivists still emphasise the role of structures over agency. Bourdieu presents an alternative:

> ... a structural constructivist account of politics that believes in the construction of reality by agents who, constrained by structures that are material and symbolic, struggle to accumulate social resources. (Kauppi, 2003, p. 777)

There is a trend (re)emerging in EU studies for research which gets closer to actors and processes in Brussels (Favell & Guiraudon, 2009, 2011; Ross, 2011). Having been 'curiously absent', 'sociology is finally being called for by mainstream studies of the EU seeking new inspiration' (Favell & Guiraudon, 2011, p. 1). Medrano suggests sociologists have neglected the EU because they do not see a 'society' there (Jenson & Mérand, 2010, p. 80). However, like Abélès I found in the EP, 'a closed world with its own codes and ways of doing things' (1993, p. 1). A sociological approach means seriously exploring the practices of actors in social spaces (Georgakakis, 2010, p. 85; Mérand, 2011, p. 188). It enables exploration of resources, positions of agents, and professional trajectories, and the building of a new picture of the way the institutions are set up and work. Institutions are not seen as an organigram or list of rules but 'as a space of people ordered by the unequal distribution of their capital' (Georgakakis, 2011, p. 333). This broadens the scope of analysis beyond the usual variables of statistical analysis. Studies approach integration from the 'bottom up' at the level of everyday political life (Kauppi, 2003, p. 776) and focus on the formation of a distinct European field of action and power struggles (Favell & Guiraudon, 2011, pp. 18–23).

Although a systematic mapping of the EU field is yet to be implemented, a growing number of case studies exist (Georgakakis, 2011, p. 331). Kauppi (2011) explores MEPs' profiles, resources, and uneven professionalization. He finds the limited political value of the EP has enabled dominated groups and novices to build their political careers and legitimize side-lined issues. Certain resources and characteristics are necessary to reach the top of the field and Kauppi highlights the development of (European) professionalization and endogenous specialisation among MEPs. He notes that individuals still behave in manners characteristic of their national political cultures. Beauvallet and Michon (2010) use MEPs' biographies to analyse professionalization and socialisation and also underline the emergence of specialists who dominate the parliamentary space. They find the emergence of a parliamentary elite occupying the EP's leadership positions with specific European resources, capital, and career types. They find MEPs often have less legitimate resources than national politicians and that the EP represents an opportunity for political professionalization. These accounts make clear that 'the EU does not do anything by itself; it is people as everyday political agents who make the EU happen' (Kauppi, 2011, p. 150).

This ethnographic study draws inspiration from this research strand and explores the everyday practice of European politics by people accumulating resources in this transnational field and power struggles between them, to enhance our understanding of MEP behaviour, beyond RCVs. A more sociological approach leads to a different interpretation of politics and shares many of the concerns of EU anthropology (Favell & Guiraudon, 2011, pp. 1–4). Some anthropology was conducted in the 1990s by those who saw political actors as socially embedded (Demossier, 2011; Abélès, 1993; Abélès et al., 2010; Bellier, 2000; Shore, 2000; Zabusky, 1995; Ross, 1995).

Part of the resurging qualitative tradition, ethnography studies actors in their setting, contextual factors, and seeks to understand actors on their own terms – the emic perspective (Denzin & Lincoln, 1998; Eriksen, 2001). By spending a sustained amount of time living in a field-site among one's informants, ethnography enables research to focus on everyday activities, routines, and perspectives. It requires the researcher to take a holistic approach to the context and take anything into account participants reveal as important (O'Reilly, 2009, p. 122; Gellner & Hirsch, 2001, p. 7; Cerwonka & Malkki, 2007; Ybema et al., 2009). This immersion gives access to everyday practices and unarticulated attitudes which go unquestioned as they are local common sense which is taken for granted and therefore has a real impact on the way politics is practised (Schatzberg, 2008). Instead of seeking predictable and rational outcomes of negotiations and decision-making, Wodak argues scholars should approach doing politics as 'highly context dependent, influenced by national traditions and politics systems, by the habitus of politicians, the modes of performance, the many embodied personality features, organisational structures and antagonistic political interests' (2009, p. 26). This paper demonstrates that intensive ethnographic fieldwork confronting the empirical world coupled with a Bourdieusian theoretical framework which approaches the EP as a transnational field, can help make roles, motives, and resources more visible and hence help us gain a more nuanced understanding of MEP behaviour, by putting *people* and *meaning* back into political analysis (Vromen, 2010, p. 253; Schatz, 2009; Ringe, 2010, p. 3; Wodak, 2009; Crewe, 2005, p. 6).

Bourdieu: A Sociological Theoretical Framework for Analysis

Ethnography can be coupled with Bourdieu's political theory for a sociological analysis. Whilst a growing number of scholars are using Bourdieu's concepts to analyse the EU, Adler-Nissen's work is particularly inspiring for those exploring behaviour inside an EU institution. Investigating marginalisation processes and the consequences of opting out for the position of member states, she presents the Council as a transnational field where opt-outs are managed on a daily basis among a body of national representatives who share a particular habitus. In this field, there is a struggle for power to define new legislation and projects, and an opt-out can be seen as a *stigma* which leads to *stigma management strategies* being pursued by diplomats (2009, pp. 22–23). Political sociology focuses on 'the study of power and the junction of personality, social structure and politics' (Adler-Nissen, 2009, p. 80) and thus is a fruitful approach to the EP; an institution where members have continuously battled for more powers (Priestley, 2008). Bourdieu's theory presents a fertile approach for exploring the implications of structures, as it enables the investigation of power structures and the historical and cultural contexts in which they gain social meaning. This is increasingly important in Brussels where the rules of the game are not all codified and 'many operate through informal processes that rely on cultural competence and symbolic capital' (Shore, cited in Mundell, 2010).

Structural Constructivism

Bourdieu's structural constructivism is an interdisciplinary approach which transcends the artificial division between structure and agency and allows us to explore how social meaning is generated and has consequences. This midway theory breaks with the presuppositions of structuralism which disregards social actors' capacity for creativity and intention, without relapsing into individualism, and allows space for structure and agency in analysis (Bourdieu, 1990, p. 61). This interpretivist account of politics sees actors as constrained by material and symbolic structures, struggling to accumulate social resources, and is Durkheimian in its holistic approach and Weberian in its approach to political processes in economic terms and concentration on capital (Kauppi, 2003, pp. 777–780). It assumes social reality is constructed in an on-going, dynamic process and reproduced by people acting on their interpretations of reality, and social meanings are generated around structures, so constraints are socially produced. Structures come to have meaning for people which reflect an institution's social history and lead to particular structures of symbolic power which 'provide strong situational logics of action' but do not determine behaviour. In the relationship between habitus and field, 'the crucial aspect of this equation is *relationship between*, because neither habitus nor field has the capacity to unilaterally determine social action' (Wacquant, 2006, cited in Adler-Nissen, 2009, p. 85). Structures have an impact through actors' interpretation of their social meaning. Practice is central to this venture and Bourdieu was oriented towards micro-sociological practices, studied in order to understand how structures, particularly power structures, are reproduced and transformed in practice (Webb et al., 2002, p. 36). Ethnographic data about everyday practices viewed through the lens of the following concepts, enables a more nuanced discussion about the relationship between structures and actors' behaviour.

Field

Field, a key concept in Bourdieu's toolbox, is defined as 'a structured system of social positions – occupied by either individuals or institutions – the nature of which defines the situation for their occupants' (Jenkins, 2002, p. 85). Thinking in terms of fields means thinking about social spaces so a specific, de-limited space becomes the centre of the analysis rather than a group (Barnard, 1990). Adler-Nissen defines the field as:

> ... a relatively autonomous social system consisting of a patterned set of practices and beliefs, which suggests competent action in conformity with rules and roles. A

field is a historically derived system of shared meanings which define agency and
make action intelligible. (Adler-Nissen, 2009, p. 87)

Within this relatively autonomous site, certain behaviour is regarded as appropriate and individuals develop a sense of the social game. Many fields exist and each is divided into sub-fields. Within the field, individuals compete for certain types of capital, which the stratification of the field is based upon. As well as a structured system of positions, the field is also 'a system of forces which exist between these positions' which relate to each other in dominance, subordination, and equivalence by the access they have to the capital at stake (Jenkins, 2002, p. 85). We can think of political behaviour in and through the field where stakes are defined and positions distributed and where a particular struggle takes place which is relatively autonomous from the member states. Georgakakis says the EU field:

... is the concrete space of routine delegation where policies are built and political outputs constructed... understood as a space of relationships between agents who, from their institutional position or not, are competing for the definition of European institutions and policies. (Georgakakis, 2010, p. 113)

We can therefore explore the EP as a social system which follows its own laws and logics (Adler-Nissen, 2009, p. 90).

Capital

Their position, and type and amount of capital give actors influence within the field (Webb et al., 2002, p. 23). The field creates in the participants a belief in the legitimacy and value of the capital at stake and all fields have an unequal distribution of capital which is accepted by actors. Capital is derived from the resources which count as valid currency in the field and what counts as valid capital can shift over time. Actors have the chance to accumulate capital during interactions. A particular type of capital, political capital, 'involves specific social skills, the capacity to mobilize individuals around a common goal, to formulate collective policies, or to win seats' (Kauppi, 2003, p. 778). Bourdieu said of political capital: 'this supremely free-flowing capital can be conserved only at the cost of unceasing work, which is necessary both to accumulate credit and to avoid discredit' (1992 in Adler-Nissen, 2009, p. 100). Individuals' capital in the field can change over time with their choices, interactions, and strategies.

Strategies

Within the struggle for influence, actors can use their position and capital strategically which can help us understand behaviour within the field. *Strategy* is a more useful concept than rules because it encourages research to explore motivations behind strategies to avoid passing off 'the things of logic as the logic of things' (Bourdieu, 1990, p. 61). Bourdieu speaks of social action as a game, a locus of regularities, which is played by players who have learnt strategies. Mastery of the game is acquired through experience, but this still allows for infinite possibilities because actors can follow the best action in each situation. Strategies come from peoples' experiences of reality, 'their practical sense of logic' (Jenkins, 2002, pp. 70–72). This logic of practice implies that people are able to develop a feel for the game which is learned consciously and unconsciously; it is a consequence of experiencing appropriate behaviour in the field, which new members must learn in order to operate effectively. Adler-Nissen stresses that norms and strategic behaviour are not opposites; agents are capable of reflecting on their own behaviour as they adapt to new or changing environments, and they can behave strategically in an environment where there is strong socialisation. However, they do not necessarily perceive consciously that they are behaving strategically to achieve influence because the field generates its own unarticulated *sens practique*. The key to understanding this is within Bourdieu's framework where strategy is bound to the habitus (Adler-Nissen, 2009, pp. 102–104).

Habitus

Bourdieu described the habitus as a socially acquired system of dispositions which is generated by the field and learnt by exposure and experience (1990, p. 60). It is a property of social agents (individuals or groups), and a systematically ordered system of dispositions which generates perceptions (Maton, 2008, p. 51). Durable and practical, it provides the rules of the game for everyday life and standards which individuals operate within. Because the habitus is conceived of as embodied dispositions rather than rules, it allows for decisions and actions to vary across time and space. Bourdieu's (contested and controversial) definition of *disposition* is essential; he describes it as 'a way of being, a habitual state... a predisposition, tendency, propensity or inclination' (1977 in Maton, 2008, p. 51). While field and capital give us an understanding of the structures of a social system, habitus is linked directly to practice and individuals, and can help us understand how structures relate to strategies in the field. It is a key element of the reconciliation of structure and agency and attempts to answer how behaviour can be regulated without obedience to rules. Fields generate a particular habitus and certain dispositions are seen as appropriate, more likely to lead to influence, or are even required to function in the field.

The habitus is reproduced in socialisation as dispositions are taken on and its power 'derives from the thoughtlessness of habit and habituation' (Jenkins, 2002, p. 76). However, the habitus is not necessarily coherent or harmonious because it reflects individuals' histories and can change over time). Political sociology suggests notions of norm-following should be placed into a particular field, where actors' understanding of goals is pieced together by the habitus and doxa, and the supply of options develops in response to the constraints of the field's particular history (Adler-Nissen, 2009, p. 93).

Doxa

Along with the everyday internalisation of the habitus, a field also has foundational rules which actors do not even reflect upon. The doxa is the unspoken structures, taken-for-granted premise, and fundamental truth which makes co-operation meaningful for actors. Jenkins says, because actors are an integral part of their circumstances and within them they acquire practical competence, they are incapable of perceiving arbitrary social reality as 'anything other than the way things are, necessary to their own existence as *who* they are', and take their social world for granted (2002, p. 70). The doxa operates 'as if it were the objective truth', so to identify it, we must ask questions actors themselves do not even consider (Adler-Nissen, 2009, pp. 97–99). Exploring the taken for granted in the Council, Adler-Nissen found the opt-outs are thought to be a breach of solidarity and threaten the *acquis communautaire*. She suggests this attachment to the *acquis* is indicative of the doxa of the Council where laws are not just regulative but play a constitutive role in the identity formation of actors because it signifies the meaning of European co-operation; the opt-outs threaten this and hence are met with particular reaction. We can explore what is taken for granted and what this tells us about the practice of politics in the EP. As Adler-Nissen says; 'any attempt at modelling the world can be criticised for reducing complexity' (2009, p. 113). However, this dynamic theoretical scheme provides a lens through which to view detailed data to provide a deeper, more nuanced understanding of behaviour within an institutional context.

The EP as a Transnational Political Field

Within the following sections I discuss findings from data gathered via ethnographic fieldwork in 2010 which consisted of seven months participant observation and 58 elite interviews in the EP, with the application of the theoretical framework outlined, to explore the everyday practice of politics by individual MEPs within this transnational space. The data was systematically analysed with *qualitative analytical coding* which consisted of *open* and *focused coding* and writing *theoretical memos*. These analytical practices draw heavily on methods developed by those taking a grounded theory approach, who prioritise developing rather than verifying analytical propositions, making discovery of new ideas more likely (Emerson et al., 1995, pp. 142–168; Glaser & Strauss, 1967). It also focuses the analysis on the emic perspective.

Field: A Level Playing Field, or a Field with Two Levels?

I usually began the interviews by asking participants about their experience of how the EP works or its working culture, then asking MEPs and staff what it takes to be an effective MEP, how they pursue their goals, what new MEPs must learn, who interviewees thought were the most influential actors, and what their own positions involved. Many interviewees said the EP has a distinct way of working, but some found it difficult to describe. One MEP's assistant said:

> ... it is another world, you cannot imagine it. No one explains it to you exactly, and even if they do, it's not the same as actually being here, it's very different... if you don't actually work for the institutions, then you don't really understand how they work. (Interview 3)

Their responses reflected my fieldwork experience in Brussels. The 'Brussels bubble' is a small, isolated, transnational community with its own particular practices; small as people often discuss how everyone knows each other and how connected people are, and isolated or segregated as they usually only know other *eurocrats* working in the 'bubble' and no locals (Rozanska, 2011). The geography of the Brussels bubble means we can identify a specific, de-limited space in which European politics is practiced (Figure 1). We find the clustering of the EU institutions in the European Quarter with their distinctive, futuristic architecture, a smattering of historical plaques, and the ubiquitous EU symbols such as the flag. The EU constitutes 'a kind of superfield that is composed of a variety of smaller-scale, relatively autonomous fields of action' (Kauppi, 2011, p. 154) – such as

EUROPE, DISCOURSE, INSTITUTIONS

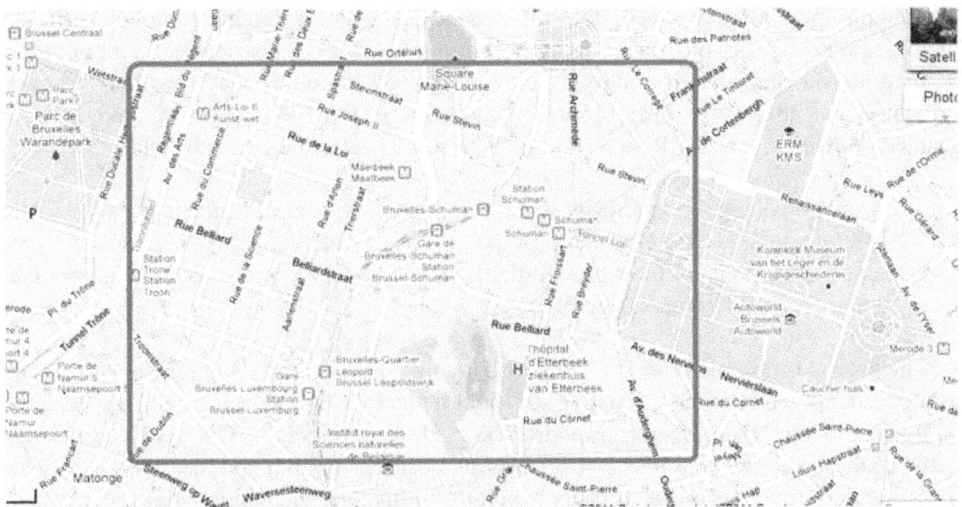

Figure 1. The Brussels bubble
Map data ©2013 Google

the EP. Fields have different habiti and can be distinguished by their different lifestyles. The EP can be distinguished from the other EU institutions by its particular rhythm of life which is guided by the daily, weekly, and monthly comings and goings of the MEPs. Those operating within this transnational field were able to identify a system of positions and practices operating within this relatively autonomous physical and social space.

Many interviewees, including all 18 of the MEPs interviewed, described the EP's co-operative, consensus culture, the extent of which had initially surprised a number of them. They highlighted the importance of working together across groups, nationalities, and delegations and of constantly building alliances in an institution where there is no permanent majority or government. One MEP said that the EP is 'very consensus oriented' and that MEPs work with respect and communication within and between the political groups, and advised that MEPs should not be 'too edgy' in their dealings with colleagues because you may disagree today but need a colleague tomorrow on another issue (Interview 7). Many also discussed the egalitarian nature of this consensus culture. The EP is a place where every individual MEP has the opportunity to make things happen because everyone is in government due to the fact that the EP is not dominated by a permanent majority and coalitions change with the issue so there are many opportunities for individuals to be involved in and influence the policy process and institutional politics – if they are prepared to put in the hard work; i.e., play the game and accumulate valid capital. The interviewees' accounts (particularly the 18 MEPs') gave the sense of a level playing field and an inclusive working culture, for those willing to play the game.

However, as interviewees discussed strategies to be an effective MEP and who they thought were influential actors in the field, another experience emerged. Interviewees regularly identified two actors they felt were influential in institutional processes; the Conference of Presidents (CoP) and committee co-ordinators. This reflects a division in individual MEPs' everyday activities, between a political and legislative sub-field which operate simultaneously inside the field (Ringe & Victor, 2013). An MEP said; 'there are two different lots of politics being played here, the stuff around the work we do and the policy stuff, but there's also the politics of who's top dog' (Interview 5). Many interviewees said building a reputation as a specialist in a narrow policy area is an important way for MEPs to exert influence and after some time observing meetings in the EP, I began to take this for granted. However, one MEP nuanced this with reference to the two sub-fields:

> I would challenge the premise, you do not necessarily have to focus on a particular topic, *if* you are in the leadership of the groups so much, this is when you steer processes more than influence a particular topic... when you're a regular member though, I would agree. (Interview 7)

The political sub-field refers to MEPs occupying political leadership positions (e.g., the group leaders), whereas the legislative sub-field refers to MEPs working daily on the detail of legislation (e.g., co-ordinators, rapporteurs, shadow rapporteurs). There is bleed-through between these sub-fields as some MEPs occupy positions in both and these two sub-fields meet regularly and negotiate, notably when co-ordinators and rapporteurs present their reports in group meetings. Often MEPs and their staff working in the legislative sub-field seemed to have little knowledge about what their group leaders did, particularly in the CoP, but they were extremely knowledgeable about their committee work. From the first month of my fieldwork, participants stressed the important and influential role co-ordinators play in decision-making processes, and the everyday practice of EP politics. Over lunch, one assistant told me enthusiastically that if I wanted to know where decisions are made, I needed to talk to co-ordinators who meet regularly with co-ordinators from other groups to allocate reports and they also meet with their group leaderships. Meanwhile, interviewees routinely identified group leaders as influential, one official describing how deals are brokered among them in the CoP (Interview 2).

Whilst this transnational political field is perceived as relatively inclusive by participants, rather than a level playing field, it is more accurately experienced as *a field with two levels*, political and legislative, where there is a structured system of positions which define the situation for occupants with power relations between them (Jenkins, 2002, p. 85) and some positions are perceived as more influential than others. As one MEP said; 'consensus is formed and the deals are struck between a relatively small group of people on each side who know how to operate in the system' (Interview 4).

Habitus: What Does It Take to Be an Effective MEP?

This point was re-iterated as I explored further how to be an effective MEP. It takes time to learn how to operate in the EP, two MEPs suggesting over two years to understand what is going on behind the scenes, and that at first the institution can be a bewildering experience (Interviews 4 and 7). There are a number of things new MEPs need to learn. This includes the role of institutional tools. One MEP initially over-estimated the importance of Written Declarations which he later realised were time-consuming and 'essentially pointless' and under-estimated the importance of speaking in plenary, an occasion when the other institutions, the entire press core, and all the EP TV screens are focused on you (Interview 7). As well as formal procedures, this transnational field generates a particular set of dispositions which designate appropriate behaviour, and MEPs hoping to influence EU legislation and EP politics have to learn to operate within them:

> ... the most important thing is to understand the culture of the place. Where some MEPs fail, is that they believe they can do this together with another job or interest, or that they can swan in at the time when you have to vote...When you've been here a while you can decide with greater knowledge how best to use your time, but if you are not prepared to throw yourself into it at the beginning, you never really understand what it's about. (Interview 4)

Initially, I asked what it takes to be a *good* MEP. MEPs usually said a good MEP listens to constituents' views and represents them in Brussels rather than becoming too detached. However, when I asked what it takes to be an *effective* MEP (removing a normative element), they revealed strategies through which they pursue their aims and interests inside the institution. Often they referred back to the EP's consensus culture and how you should approach colleagues co-operatively. It takes time to learn what behaviour is appropriate and some described how they got this wrong at first. The antithesis of the appropriate disposition for an (effective) MEP to embody was demonstrated in February 2010 by Nigel Farage when he called Council President Herman Van Rompuy a 'damp rag' from a 'non country', which was met with gasps as 'the personal attack shocked the normally consensual EP' (EurActiv, 25 February 2010). Whilst this adversarial style is typical in Westminster, it is not typical of the EP's consensual habitus. However, as Adler-Nissen says, a habitus is not necessarily harmonious and this concept allows us to explore inconsistencies; for example the adversarial disposition performed by UKIP MEPs for whom the stakes of the game are different and are playing a different game (Calhoun, 2000, pp. 274–278).

Adapting to and embodying the dispositions of the habitus is part of the socialisation process for MEPs seeking to influence EU legislation and politics. *Habitus* enables us to observe everyday behaviour and take a more nuanced approach to change and exploring what, if anything, it means to take a more *European* approach, rather than equating socialisation crudely with time spent and voting position. As Kauppi says:

> European political integration is also social and cultural integration. Spending time in Brussels changes the political habitus of politicians. For... politicians work in Brussels does not present an alternative to national political careers, they do not all become federalists after having worked in the EU. (Kauppi, 2003, p. 785)

However, to influence policy and politics whilst there, they must learn to play the game and employ their position and capital strategically within the habitus.

Capital and Strategies: Which Actors Are Most Influential?

Participant observation enabled me to observe backstage meetings and the ways decisions were reached. I observed who spoke, what they said, and reactions to them, as well as who was called upon to speak and why. In committee, group, and plenary two types of MEPs spoke most often; firstly MEPs holding a relevant formal office (e.g., group leader, co-ordinators, [shadow] rapporteurs, and committee chairs) and secondly, MEPs holding an informal reputation as a specialist. I probed this further by asking participants what they thought were the most important EP roles, who they thought had the most influence, and how they went about achieving their goals. Within this transnational field, actors can employ their position and capital strategically to influence policy and politics; signalling a distinction between individual and delegated capital. Bourdieu differentiated two types of political capital, that acquired by the individual and that by delegation. Individual capital is accumulated by the individual, either slowly or during a crisis and disappears with the individual character. Delegated capital is acquired through investiture by an institution, where an individual receives a limited and provisional transfer of collective capital when capital becomes institutionalized in positions (Kauppi, 2003 p. 780).

Holding a formal EP office (a position in the field) is an important way to influence proceedings in the EP. When asked about how to be effective, two MEPs suggested the best route is to become a full committee member of something that interests you; then a rapporteur where you learn how reports are written, what meetings take place, and how the system works; and then a committee chair (Interviews 4 and 7). EP offices give individuals access to restricted backstage meetings, documents, information, staff denied to others, and means that they will have more opportunities to arrive prepared for and influence the formal decision-making process and thinking about an issue, by speaking first, last, and more often, and perhaps also by chairing meetings, shaping agendas, and allocating speakers and tasks. Holding an office also means other actors will approach you with information and ideas. Co-ordinators, rapporteurs, and 'shadows' often speak first about the detail of a dossier and its progress, providing expertise others do not have (Ringe, 2010), and group and committee chairs often open and close debates, setting the agenda, providing the summary, and guiding the debate. Therefore these actors are regularly institutionally influential in decision-making processes.

There are a number of formal offices available, arranged within a structured system with power relations existing between them; as has been suggested, some MEPs are seen as more equal than others. One MEP summarised this concisely, again with reference to the two sub-fields:

> ... in terms of substance, the co-ordinators have a key role, because the substantive work is done at committee level, and the people who represent the group in the small meetings of the co-ordinators there, they have a large degree of influence. On the more political level, I would clearly say it's the group leader, whose job it is to hammer out common lines and agreed positions from what is of course a rather heterogeneous group of people...I'd say these are the two groups of people. (Interview 7)

These two positions were identified by numerous others. Co-ordinators are influential because they are the pivotal figure moving between the group and committee (Interview 11). With the chair they 'manage all the life of the committee collectively' (Interview 12) and they also lead on the group line and promote the committee in their group (Interview 11). Having a skilled co-ordinator, who knows how to 'do politics' and build alliances, can make a huge difference to the performance of a group within a committee in terms of getting their policy preferences into legislation because they negotiate with the other groups (Interview 5). Another co-ordinator referred to their responsibility of assigning reports to rapporteurs between and within the groups (Interview 6). Rapporteurs and shadows are key figures in the legislative field; once a report is allocated to them, they guide it through the complex institutional labyrinth, are likely to be contacted by many relevant interest groups, speak on its behalf, work with expert officials, and have access to the important meetings including eventually trialogues. They are influential among their colleagues because of the highly technical nature of EU legislation; 'you can't be a specialist in everything, you have to rely heavily on the rapporteur doing the job and hope they actually know what they're talking about' (Interview 5).

Co-ordinators play an important role in allocating these positions. One co-ordinator said it is their job to get interesting dossiers for the group in negotiations with other groups' co-ordinators, and then assign them. This can be an extremely powerful way to influence proceedings because they can compare candidates from other groups and whether they have a more European or national point of view (Interview 6). Some co-ordinators are more consensual than others in the committee prep meeting discussions. Another co-ordinator said the distribution of reports is absolutely strategic and that they look at how compromising MEPs were likely to behave for dossiers where they wanted to avoid amendments; sometimes group targets had to be let go when it seemed other groups could handle reports better (Interview 12). One MEP said that of course co-ordinators are influential and 'mightier than the others because you know a bit earlier than the others, so you can influence the direction your group goes in the committee' (Interview 6).

Meanwhile, in the *political* sub-field, the group leaders and the CoP were identified as the most influential actors in the internal life of the institution. The CoP is designated administrative tasks by the Rules of Procedure; it 'shall take decisions on the organisation of Parliament's work and matters relating to legislative planning' (Rule 25:2). It is where the group leaders regularly meet and discuss plenary. When asked about influential actors, one MEP said; 'of course, it is the CoP. I would say that this is really *the* most important political steering organ of the EP. The EP Bureau is more administrative, and deals with issues which affect the EP as an institution, but not with policies, and in that sense, the CoP is the most important at the EP level' (Interview 7).

Meanwhile, some interviewees listed certain positions as *not* influential. An MEP stressed that the Vice President, in committee and group, 'doesn't count at all, if you're talking about influence, it is completely irrelevant, it's a nice title, and you can sell it at home, but there's no influence' (Interview 8). However, he added that one group Vice President did wield significant influence because everybody respected and viewed them as extremely competent. Whilst formal positions (delegated capital) might 'define the situation for their occupants' (Jenkins, 2002, p. 85) by dictating what they can access, individuals can still manoeuvre from positions in practice using other types of valid capital; something this theoretical framework explores due to its approach to structure and agency. Once the formal offices have been doled out according to the D'Hondt procedure, an alternative strategy is to accumulate informal (individual) capital and build a reputation within this transnational community. Three important dispositions emerged; being hardworking, co-operative, and a specialist; particular to the way this field has developed historically.

When asked about influential actors, numerous MEPs and staff took a moment to name specific individual MEPs. An MEP said influential MEPs are 'clearly the group leader. It is a number of colleagues... who mostly on merit, really wield influence, because they are good at what they do and they are hard-working, and they are committed to the success of the things that they do' (Interview 7). Individuals named were those I saw speaking regularly in meetings, who had built an informal reputation. Due to the short time MEPs spend in Brussels each week (often Monday lunchtime to Thursday lunchtime), using your time effectively is crucial, as is the perception of working hard:

> ... be modest and work, here, there is no blah, blah. Here nobody knows you. You can be a former minister, you can be very famous in your country, but in the other

countries, it is very likely that no one knows you, even if you were a prime minister or some other star 10 years ago. The only way for you to be respected and to count here, is to do your work properly, to look at problems with a very modest eye, say, well we are in a team, we have to build a team and we have to listen to each other. (Interview 12)

Being co-operative is an essential disposition within this consensual habitus where constantly building shifting alliances is a crucial part of the everyday practice of politics. A reputation of being co-operative and a good negotiator enables individual MEPs to punch above their weight:

... this guy is very good at finding common ground, negotiating and bringing people together... particularly for a small political group, I mean obviously we can't achieve anything on our own, so making alliances with other political groups is crucial, a lot of that is down to personal relationships, what kind of approach you take. (Interview 1)

For individual MEPs, and particularly those in smaller groups, a reputation as a policy specialist can be important:

... we punch much above our weight... the Greens were looked at as people with expertise... there's an MEP from Luxembourg, who I think anybody would agree is the Parliament's expert on energy, even if you don't agree with him, people would respect the fact he is deeply immersed in his subject and knows it completely in depth... we've had a much bigger impact on the shape of the Parliament, the way in which the majorities go, than some other MEPs that are there. (Interview 1)

In the legislative sub-field, committing to a topic and building a reputation as a specialist can be an important strategy. Specialisation can be built through knowledge from a previous career or from scratch inside the institution. One MEP said:

... the people who achieve the most here, are those who specialise in and therefore become specialists in, a very, very narrow range of issues. Those who are interested by lots of things and dabble in lots of things, tend not to get to the heart of any matter, but those who specialise... end up determining the shape of policy. (Interview 4)

This is due to the highly technical nature of EU legislation which means no individual MEP can know everything about every report and the hundreds of amendments they vote on each plenary. It is also due to the avalanche of information MEPs receive, an office receiving nearly 200 emails every day; the information overload can be 'mind-boggling' (Interview 7). Specialists are therefore influential because, as one MEP said; 'so I have very high respect for our specialists for our different areas, so you cannot know everything, it is too much, so you have to go along with your group' (Interview 10). Ringe also suggests MEPs lack adequate resources to make decisions in every policy area and therefore follow their expert colleague from the relevant committee with whom they have *perceived preference coherence* (2010). In this transnational field, MEPs trust and rely on each others' expertise, a valid form of capital and an important strategy for those seeking to influence policy. As an assistant told me during fieldwork, to understand EP politics, you have to look at all the work that precedes a plenary vote; activities which become visible when we open the institutional black-box and explore everyday activities and actors' perspectives.

Doxa: Performing Multiple Interests

Whilst talking with actors can be revealing and insightful, research must also interrogate their responses as they may be offering a validating account of themselves, their role, lifestyle, institution, and politics (Ball, 1994, p. 99). Critical analysis is essential to explore the doxa; an institution's unarticulated *sens practique*. Anthropology can help reveal taken for granted practices which participants don't regard worth commenting on, even though they shape the everyday practice of politics (in Mundell, 2010). One MEP told me after our interview that he thought he had not told me anything interesting, despite me finding the discussion about his institutional role and tactics he employs to achieve aims after being in the EP for many years, very illuminating (Interview 9).

The doxa is the 'fundamental truth which makes co-operation meaningful for the actors within the context' (Adler-Nissen, 2009, p. 97). Much of the quantitative EP research tries to determine the variable which most accurately predicts voting behaviour and explains institutional outcomes. However, spending close and sustained time in this field among its transnational elite, observing everyday activities and backstage processes, suggests that in practice MEPs negotiate a myriad of interests and perform multiple roles on a daily basis. Analysing an MEP's diary schedule and observing their everyday activities for seven months, showed that many MEPs perform different roles and represent different interests on a daily basis. This is firstly due to the EP's monthly calendar which designates roughly a week per month to groups, committees, plenary, and constituencies, which means these four priorities are formally institutionalised to regularly receive MEPs' attention. Secondly, on a daily basis, MEPs perform different roles in the meetings they hold with interest groups, constituents, EP officials, and group colleagues. They embody different roles in the different meetings they attend and speak on behalf of different interests to convince others of their views and position. Co-operation among actors in this field is meaningful, and possible, because they all embody this complex task, balancing interests and performing multiple roles in this transnational space.

MEPs are 'faced with cross-cutting multiple identities… they also have an institutional identity fashioned by the decision rules of the Union that force the EP to negotiate with the Council on legislative output' (Laffan, 2004, p. 94). Over lunch, a lobbyist told me I had come to the EP at an interesting time. Since Lisbon he had noticed MEPs becoming more confident in their relations with the other institutions. One interest which is fundamental to the identity of participants in this field is the EP's institutional identity in relation to the other EU institutions. This has been crucial in its long quest for power (Priestley, 2008) where a collective institutional interest has been apparent. Ripoll Servent says:

> … this overall objective is at the core of the institutional preferences of the EP and thus works as the normative point of reference. Obviously policy preferences vary… however, they will have fewer chances to succeed if they contradict this primary institutional interest' (Ripoll Servent, 2011, p. 8)

A number of interviewees alluded to ways in which the internal dynamics of the EP are shaped by its position in the EU triangle. To complete an earlier quotation, one MEP said:

> ... there are two different lots of politics being played here, the stuff around the work we do and the policy stuff, but there's also the politics of who's top dog in this place, the agenda the pro-Europeans have, how do we get more power for the parliament. (Interview 5)

The historical development of the EU and institutional context in which the EP finds itself, shapes the field and the habitus which has developed within it. It has contributed to the consensus culture, two-level field, and role of key actors. One MEP, ruminating on how he had found the extent of the consensus culture surprising, said:

> Yes it's quite unique that you have this consensus parliament. The reason why we make broad compromises is that we know in this House that we have no influence if we don't because our counterpart is the Commission and the Council and if we don't have a broad majority, well they just tell us, well you don't agree anyway in the parliament so go to hell with your papers. (Interview 8)

This priority appears within the legislative sub-field where the need to consider the position of the EP vis-à-vis the other institutions encourages co-operation, consensus, and alliance building, showing that the doxa penetrates the institution. As a co-ordinator said, they divide the reports in a sensitive way to try to strengthen the role of the parliament as a whole, because we know that from the outside we are not just seen as ALDE, either the parliament has an influence or we lose collectively, so it's always a strange game between defending our political visions, and at the same time entering a logic of co-operation with the others (Interview 12).

However this was more apparent within the political sub-field. The doxa naturalises itself, operating as if it were objective truth and becoming a fundamental part of participants' identity (Jenkins, 2002, p. 70). Naturalisation of the doxa was apparent in this MEP's discussion of the CoP:

> ... it is a very strange body really... for the preparation of certain strategic political decisions...it can't stray too far... but there is of course the particular European aspect to consider, this parliament is an institution in the institutional triangle; the consensus based approach and the requirement for a qualified majority in the second readings, *forces*, really *forces* at least the centre of this house to co-operate... it's only natural, that's the set up, the treaty based set up of this parliament, and that in my view, explains and justifies the existence of the CoP. (Interview 7)

Whilst the groups often fight along ideological lines (Hix et al., 2007), there are times when the EP's institutional identity takes priority. The internal impact of collective, institutional identity has been explored by other scholars (Kreppel, cited in McElroy, 2006, p. 179; Farrell & Héritier, 2004; Ripoll Servent, 2012, 2011; Ripoll Servent & MacKenzie, p. 2011). This idea resonates with what Parker has said more broadly about organisations, that:

> ... organizational cultures should be seen as *fragmented unities* in which members identify themselves as collective at some times and divided at others... [it] should be understood as involving both the everyday understandings of members and the more general features of the sector, state and society. (Parker, 2000, p. 1)

The theoretical and methodological approach outlined in this paper enable a more nuanced approach to be taken to understanding behaviour occurring inside this institution. Such research can make a contribution to the EP literature, which currently takes 'too broad a brush' and misses some important elements of the practice of politics such as everyday processes and perspectives (Ringe, 2010, p. 2), to which this approach attends and which is therefore its added value.

Concluding Remarks

Structural constructivism enables us to take a more holistic approach to institutions such as the EP and explore a transnational political space where activities and processes occur, as a field which constrains and enables behaviour of actors operating within it. Whilst the EP has increasingly attracted academic attention and quantitative research has significantly contributed to explaining outcomes, there is now a gap which calls for more sociological research which pays closer attention to internal processes and the everyday practice of politics by actors. The theoretical and methodological approach outlined offers a contribution to this endeavour as it pays close attention to everyday activities, backstage processes, meaning, and actors' perspectives which enables us to explore how they understand their context, meanings they attribute to it, and to behaviour within it – to begin addressing the under-socialised nature of the literature.

This approach has shown us that the EP is perceived as a co-operative, egalitarian, and inclusive institution. However whilst actors were keen to stress the consensus culture, their stories suggest, rather than a level playing field, it is perhaps more accurately experienced as a field with two levels, political and legislative, where some positions are more influential than others in each of the two levels. To operate successfully, MEPs acquire a co-operative disposition and are not too edgy in their dealings with colleagues. MEPs perceived as influential by colleagues had accumulated valid delegated and individual political capital, by either acquiring particular offices (in particular group leader or co-ordinator in the political or legislative sub-field respectively), or by building a reputation as a hard-working, co-operative specialist. Co-operation between MEPs with an array of specialisations and interests is meaningful because all MEPs constantly negotiate multiple interests and perform multiple roles, implying more than one variable explaining their behaviour. The institutional identity of MEPs has been important due to the historical development of the EU institutional triangle, and this context has shaped the EP field and its consensus-oriented habitus. Conceptualising the EP as a transnational political field, as a particular space in which a struggle occurs within a system of power-related positions with a habitus of particular, historically-informed dispositions and where a particular doxa operates, allows us to explore the strategies actors employ with valid capital within the context – and hence begin gaining a deeper and more nuanced understanding of individuals' behaviour within the Brussels bubble.

Interviews Cited

1	7\3\09	MEP
2	20\7\10	EP official
3	29\7\10	MEP's senior assistant
4	17\11\10	MEP, Delegation Chair

5	2\12\10	MEP, Co-ordinator
6	7\12\10	MEP, Co-ordinator
7	8\12\10	MEP
8	15\12\10	MEP, National Delegation Leader
9	15\12\10	MEP, Co-ordinator
10	15\12\10	MEP
11	15\12\10	MEP, Co-ordinator
12	16\12\10	MEP, Co-ordinator

Acknowledgements

This work was supported by the UK Economic and Social Research Council doctoral funding scheme [grant number: ES/I/900934/1].

References

Abélès, M. (1993) Political anthropology of a transnational institution: The European Parliament, *French Politics & Society*, 11(1), pp. 1–19.

Abélès, M., Bellier, I. & McDonald, M. (2010) An anthropological approach to the European Commission, Version 1–29, pp. 1–69. Available at http://Hal.archives-ouvertes.fr/docs/00/46/77/68/PDF/ABELES_BELLIER_mcdonald_EUROPEAN_COMMISSION_HAL.pdf (accessed 23 January 2013).

Adler-Nissen, R. (2008) The diplomacy of opting-out: A Bourdieudian approach to national integration strategies, *Journal of Common Market Studies*, 46(3), pp. 663–684.

Adler-Nissen, R. (2009) *The Diplomacy of Opting Out: British and Danish stigma management in the EU* (PhD thesis, Copenhagen: University of Copenhagen).

Bale, T. & Taggart, P. (2006) First timers yes, virgins no: The roles and backgrounds of new members of the European Parliament, *Sussex European Institute Working Paper 89*. Available at: http://www.sussex.ac.uk/sei/publications/seiworkingpapers (accessed 26 January 2013).

Ball, S. (1994) Political interviews and the politics of interviewing, in: G. Walford (Ed.) *Researching the Powerful in Education* (London: UCL Press).

Barnard, H. (1990) Bourdieu and ethnography: Reflexivity, politics and praxis, in: R. Harker, C. Mahar & C. Wilkes (Eds) *An Introduction to the Work of Pierre Bourdieu*, p. 58 (Hampshire: Palgrave Macmillan).

Beauvallet, W. & Michon, S. (2010) Professionalization and socialization of the members of the European Parliament, *French Politics*, 8(2), pp. 116–144.

Bellier, I. (2000) The EU, identity politics and the logic of interests' representation, in: I. Bellier & T. Wilson (Eds) *An Anthropology of the EU: Building, imagining and experiencing the new Europe*, p. 53 (Oxford: Berg).

Bourdieu, P. (1989) *In Other Words: Essays towards a reflexive sociology* (Cambridge: Polity Press).

Bourdieu, P. (1990) *The Logic of Practice* (Trans. Richard Nice) (Cambridge: Polity Press).

Bourne, A. & Cini, M. (Eds) (2005) *Palgrave Advances in European Union Studies* (Hampshire: Palgrave Macmillan).

Calhoun, C. (2000) Pierre Bourdieu, in: G. Ritzer (Ed.) *The Blackwell Companion to Major Contemporary Social Theorists*, pp. 274–309 (Oxford: Blackwell Publishing).

Cerwonka, A. & Malkki, L. (2007) *Improvising Theory: Process and temporality in ethnographic fieldwork* (Chicago: The University of Chicago Press).

Crewe, E. (2005) *Lords of Parliament: Manners, rituals and politics* (Manchester: Manchester University Press).

Demossier, M. (2011) Anthropologists and the study of the EU: Trends and debates. Paper presented at the UACES 41st Annual Conference, Cambridge, 5–7 September. Available at http://www.uaces.org/pdf/papers/1101/demossier.pdf (accessed 23 January 2013).

Denzin, N. & Lincoln, Y. (1998) Entering the field of qualitative research, in: N. Denzin & Y. Lincoln (Eds) *Collecting and Interpreting Qualitative Materials*, pp. 1–5 (London: Sage).

Emerson, R., Fretz, R. & Shaw, L. (1995) *Writing Ethnographic Fieldnotes* (Chicago: The University of Chicago Press).

Eriksen, T. H. (2001) *Small Places, Large Issues: An introduction to social and cultural anthropology* (2nd edn) (London: Pluto Press).

EurActiv (2010) British Eurosceptic insults EU president in Parliament. Available at http://www.euractiv.com/en/future-eu/british-eurosceptic-insults-eu-president-parliament-news-286011 on 4/6/2011 (accessed 23 January 2013).
European Parliament (2009) Rule 25: Duties of the Conference of Presidents, in *Rules of Procedure*. Available at http://www.europarl.europa.eu/sides/getDoc.do?pubRef=-//EP//TEXT+RULES-EP+20090714+RULE-025+DOC+XML+V0//EN&language=EN&navigationBar=YES (accessed 18 February 2012).
Farrell, H. & Héritier, A. (2004) Interorganizational negotiation and intraorganizational power in shared decision-making: Early agreements under codecision and their impact on the European Parliament and Council, *Comparative Political Studies*, 37(10) pp. 1184–1212.
Favell, A. & Guiraudon, V. (2009) The sociology of the European Union: An agenda, *European Union Politics*, 10 (4), pp. 550–576.
Favell, A. & Guiraudon, V. (Eds) (2011) *Sociology of the European Union* (Hampshire: Palgrave Macmillan).
Forsey, M. (2004) 'He's not a spy; he's one of us': Ethnographic positioning in a middle class setting, in: L. Hume & J. Mulcock (Eds) *Anthropologists in the Field: Cases in participant observation*, pp. 59–70 (New York: Columbia University Press).
Gellner, D. & Hirsch, E. (2001) Introduction: Ethnography of organisations and organisations of ethnography, in: D. Gellner & E. Hirsch (Eds) *Inside Organizations: Anthropologists at work*, p. 1 (Oxford: Berg).
Georgakakis, D. (2009) The historical and political sociology of the European Union: A uniquely French methodological approach?, *French Politics*, 7(3/4), pp. 437–455.
Georgakakis, D. (2010) Symposium introduction: French historical and political sociology of the EU: Some theoretical and methodological challenges for institutional analysis, *French Politics*, 8(2), pp. 111–115.
Georgakakis, D. (2011) Don't throw out the 'Brussels bubble' with the bathwater: From EU institutions to the field of Eurocracy, *International Political Sociology*, 5(3), pp. 331–334.
Glaser, B. & Strauss, A. (1967) *The Discovery of Grounded Theory: Strategies for qualitative research*, 46(1) (Chicago: Aldine).
Hilmer, J. (2011) Book reviews, *Acta Politica*, 46(1), pp. 98–101.
Hix, S., Raunio, T. & Scully, R. (2003) Fifty years on: Research on the European Parliament, *Journal of Common Market Studies*, 41(2), pp. 191–202.
Hix, S., Noury, A. & Roland, G. (2007) *Democratic Politics and the European Parliament* (Cambridge: Cambridge University Press).
Jenkins, Richard. (2002) 'Practice, Habitus and Field' in Pierre Bourdieu (2nd edition) (Routledge: London).
Jenson, J. & Mérand, F. (2010) Sociology, institutionalism and the European Union, *Comparative European Politics*, 8(1), pp. 74–92.
Kauppi, N. (2003) Bourdieu's political sociology and the politics of European integration, *Theory and Society*, 32 (5/6), pp. 775–789.
Kauppi, N. (2011) EU politics, in: A. Favell & V. Guiraudon (Eds) *Sociology of the European Union*, pp. 150–171 (Hampshire: Palgrave Macmillan).
Laffan, B. (2004) The EU and its institutions as identity builder, in: R. Herrmann, T. Risse & M. Brewer (Eds) *Transnational Identities: Becoming European in the EU*, pp. 75–96 (London: Rowman & Littlefields).
McElroy, G. (2006) Legislative politics, in: K. E. Jorgensen, M. Pollack & B. Rosamond (Eds) *Handbook of European Union Politics*, (London: Sage).
Maton, K. (2008) Habitus, in: M. Grenfall (Ed.) *Pierre Bourdieu: Key concepts*, pp. 175–194 (Durham: Acumen).
Mérand, F. (2011) EU policies, in: A. Favell & V. Guiraudon (Eds) *Sociology of the European Union*, pp. 172–192 (Palgrave Macmillan: Hampshire).
Mundell, I. (2010) An ethnographic perspective, *European Voice*. Available at http://www.europeanvoice.com/article/imported/an-ethnographic-perspective-/69166.aspx (accessed 15 February 2011).
O'Reilly, J. (2009) *Key Concepts in Ethnography* (London: Sage).
Parker, M. (2000) *Organizational Culture and Identity: Unity and division at work* (London: Sage).
Priestley, J. (2008) *Six Battles that Shaped Europe's Parliament* (London: John Harper Publishing).
Ringe, N. (2010) *Who Decides, and How? Preferences, Uncertainty and Policy Choice in the European Parliament* (Oxford: Oxford University Press).
Ringe, N. & Victor, J. N. (2013) *Bridging the Information Gap: Legislative member organizations as social networks in the United States and the European Union* (Michigan: University of Michigan Press).
Ripoll Servent, A. (2011) Co-decision in the European Parliament: Comparing rationalist and constructivist explanations of the Returns Directive, *Journal of Contemporary European Research*, 7(1), pp. 3–22.

Ripoll Servent, A. (2012) Playing the co-decision game? Rules' changes and institutional adaptation at the LIBE Committee, *Journal of European Integration*, 34(1), pp. 55–73.

Ripoll Servent, A. & MacKenzie, A. (2011) The battle over SWIFT: The European Parliament's consent to international agreements. Paper presented at the conference 'Supranational Governance and European Security', University of Salford, 27–28 January, pp. 215–224.

Rosen, M. (1991) Coming to terms with the field: Understanding and doing organizational ethnography, *Journal of Management Studies*, 28(1), pp. 1–24.

Ross, G. (1995) *Jacques Delors and European Integration* (Cambridge: Polity Press).

Ross, G. (2011) Postscript: Arriving late at the EU studies ball, in: A. Favell & V. Guiraudon (Eds) *Sociology of the European Union*, (Hampshire: Palgrave Macmillan).

Rozanska, J. (2011) Polish EU officials in Brussels: Analysis of an emerging community, *Migracijske i etničke teme*, 27(2), pp. 263–298. Available at http://hrcak.srce.hr/index.php?show=toc&id_broj=5999 (accessed 27 January 2013).

Schatz, E. (Ed) (2009) *Political Ethnography: What immersion contributes to the study of power* (Chicago: University of Chicago Press).

Schatzberg, M. (2008) Seeing the invisible, hearing silence, thinking the unthinkable: The advantages of ethnographic immersion, *Political Methodology: Committee on Concepts and Methods: Working Paper Series 18*. Available at http://www.concepts-methods.org/working_papers/20081201_02_PM%2018%20Schatzberg.pdf (accessed 1 March 2010).

Scully, R. (2005) *Becoming Europeans? Attitudes, behaviour and socialisation in the European Parliament* (Oxford: Oxford University Press).

Shore, C. (2000) *Building Europe: The cultural politics of European integration* (London: Routledge).

Vromen, A. (2010) Debating methods: Rediscovering qualitative methods, in: D. March & G. Stoker (Eds) *Theory and Methods in Political Science* (3rd edn) pp. 249–266 (Hampshire: Palgrave Macmillan).

Webb, J., Schirato, T. & Danaher, G. (2002) *Understanding Bourdieu* (London: Sage).

Wodak, R. (2009) *The Discourse of Politics in Action: Politics as usual* (Hampshire: Palgrave Macmillan).

Ybema, S., Yanow, D., Wels, H. & Kamsteeg, F. (Eds) (2009) *Organizational Ethnography: Studying the complexities of everyday life* (London: Sage).

Yordanova, N. (2011) The European Parliament: In need of a theory, *European Union Politics*, 12(4), pp. 597–617.

Zabusky, S. (1995) *Launching Europe: An ethnography of European cooperation in space science* (Princeton: Princeton University Press).

Coordinative Discourses in Brussels: An Agency-oriented Model of EU Foreign Policy Analysis

NIKOLA TOMIĆ
Department of Politics, History and International Relations, Loughborough University, UK

ABSTRACT *Foreign policy analysis (FPA) in a classical sense entails focusing on agents (individuals or groups of individuals). In the case of the European Union (EU), FPA becomes more problematic. Firstly, the question arises of what a foreign policy of the EU really means. This article defines EU foreign policy in a wider sense, namely along the lines of what is known as EU's external action. It focuses however on the security aspect of the EU's external action – the Common Foreign and Security Policy (CFSP) and its defence dimension, the Common Security and Defence Policy (CSDP). Furthermore, a problem of identifying agents arises in the EU setting in large part because of the complex institutional setup of the CFSP/CSDP. Although final decisions are made at the level of the Council, the policy itself is drafted and prepared at lower levels of policy-making (working parties, committees and agencies) based in Brussels. This article proposes a discursive institutionalist model of analysis, applicable to any organization of the policy process. After presenting the model's ontological and epistemological positions, as well as theoretical underpinnings, the article elaborates on the different levels of information processing and meaning construction by actors and their role in setting the overall foreign policy discourse by shaping the coordinative discourses[1] during this early phase of the policy-making process.*

Introduction

A review of the literature reveals inconsistency in the conceptualization of EU foreign policy and the more or less accurate interchangeable use of the term with terms such as 'European foreign policy', 'EU external relations' and 'EU external action'. Considering that the increasingly widespread understanding of a EU foreign policy being 'more than the CFSP', and the current use in EU everyday practice of the term 'EU external action', the article defines EU foreign policy along the lines of what is understood as

EU external action (both in the literature and the relevant EU documents). This definition consequently openly acknowledges the existence of an EU foreign policy.

Furthermore, if an EU foreign policy exists, the question arises of how to study it. The obvious answer is found in a subfield of international relations, the field of foreign policy analysis (FPA). The different approaches to FPA provide for ample epistemological and methodological choice. Considering the recent developments in FPA (see Carlsnaes, 2005) and following the developments in IR theory, a constructivist and discursive approach can provide for more detailed insight in the decision-making processes of the EU's foreign policy. Discourse analysts of EU foreign policy argue for a structure-oriented approach and against an agent-oriented approach, like the cognitive and psychological approach. On the other hand, an agency-oriented, micro and/or mid-level of analysis is more useful in the EU context due to the complexity of the institutional setup of EU foreign policy structures. The choice however does not have to be between a discursive, but structure-oriented approach on the one hand and an agency-oriented psychological/cognitive or bureaucratic politics approach on the other. This article argues that a combination of these two approaches in the EU foreign policy context is possible.

Finally, the complexity of the EU foreign policy institutional setup inevitably raises the question of the role of institutions. By following the policy-making process, an analyst encounters a complex and ever-changing process of coordination between and within institutions. Institutions in the narrow sense, closer to the formal understanding of organizations, possess a certain logic of behavior, which influences actors' formation of preferences and in end-effect their policy decisions. In the context of EU foreign policy, the different participating institutions have different roles and different degrees of influence on the policy-making process.

Formally, *de jure*, EU foreign policy decisions are made at the level of the Council. However, these decisions are made based on policy provisions, decisions, scenarios, assumptions and ideas determined by lower level Brussels-based actors in the institutional framework of the CFSP/CSDP.

These actors, who are members of committees, working groups and agencies, although receiving a set of instructions from member states, are the ones that have *de facto* power of controlling the discourse of the whole EU. They do this by materializing policies in the form of text. This text and the discourse it creates are moved up the policymaking process up to the negotiating table, and if approved, these policies are also implemented. While in the process the text and wording may change, the discourse is mostly preserved.

This article presents a model of EU foreign policy analysis, which takes into account both structuralist and constructivist assumptions as well as discursive agency-oriented approaches. These assumptions will be combined with elements from institutionalist approaches. Such an inclusive model can then be applied to any institution of the EU foreign policy institutional setup. The proposed model aims to help understand the importance of coordination and in particular the importance of coordinative discourses on the EU foreign policy process.

The article starts with an overview of the literature on the conceptualization of EU foreign policy. Once EU foreign policy is conceptualized, the article addresses the question of how to analyze EU foreign policy. After reviewing foreign policy analysis approaches, the article presents the theoretical basis of the model and finally describes in more detail the different elements of the analytical model.

EU Foreign Policy and Foreign Policy Analysis

When theorizing a phenomenon and entering into academic debates it is crucial to avoid debating definitions. If a debate has different definitions of the object addressed then the debate has no constructive resolution. That said, debating the EU's foreign policy is no different. The literature remains unclear about what one can label EU foreign policy. The literature identifies three distinct differentiations of EU foreign policy. The first view is that EU foreign policy is synonymous to the Common Foreign and Security Policy (CFSP) and its security dimension, the Common Security and Defence Policy (CSDP) – policies of the second pillar of the old EU structure. The second view is that EU foreign policy includes the CFSP/CSDP but also all aspects of EU policies from the EU's former first and third pillars that deal with third countries. These policies fall under the wider term 'external relations' of the EU and include foreign trade, international aid and development policy as well as asylum policy and immigration from third world countries. A more recent term, 'external action', is used to encompass all the policies mentioned under the description of the second view. The third view is a skeptical one and argues that the EU does not possess a foreign policy of its own but encapsulates the foreign policies of all or groups of its member states (MS). More recent variations of this view give more credit to EU's ability to have an impact on third countries and incorporate elements of EU's foreign policy, but remain stalwart in denying the EU a foreign policy in its own right. Studies closer to the third view prefer to use the term 'European foreign policy' instead of 'EU foreign policy'.

To conceptualize the EU's foreign policy, one needs to understand the subtle differences between EU foreign policy and European foreign policy, EU foreign policy and EU MS foreign policies, EU foreign policy and EU external relations and finally between EU foreign policy and EU external action. The following sub-sections will be structured accordingly.

EU Foreign Policy, European Foreign Policy and the Sum of MS Foreign Policies

It has become a habit both in the public and media as well as in academia to use 'European' and 'EU' interchangeably, like for example 'European diplomacy' vis-à-vis 'EU diplomacy' or 'European foreign policy' vis-à-vis 'EU foreign policy' While the difference may seem minuscule at first, a second closer look reveals a considerable impact on the object of research, set of research questions and theoretical approaches. When one talks of European foreign policy, one can be talking of both the foreign policy actions of the EU, as well as foreign policies of individual member states or group of member states. However, if one discusses EU foreign policy, it is clear that one is referring to the EU as the actor involved, and to all the institutional, legal, political and normative characteristics of the EU and its foreign policy. As an example, the EU does not have an official foreign policy position on the status of Kosovo, due to five of its member states not recognizing Kosovo's independence. The EU's status neutrality has institutional legal and normative consequences on EU foreign policy, but does not limit individual member states' foreign policies towards Kosovo. Simply put, the term 'European foreign policy' is more general and imprecise, which is why this article operates with the term 'EU foreign policy'.

One of the abovementioned views on EU foreign policy is that it is synonymous with the CFSP. From such a viewpoint, using the term 'EU foreign policy' is restrictive as some authors have pointed out. (White, 2004; Hill, 1998) White suggests that instead the term 'European foreign policy' should be used to 'enable studies of members states' foreign policy to be undertaken without assuming or implying that national foreign policy can now be entirely subsumed within CFSP' (White, 2004, p. 13).

Hill (1998, 2004) points out that if one defines European foreign policy solely as 'behavior of the EU in the form of the Common Foreign and Security Policy' one excludes from the definition elements of 'pillar I/Community institutions and the national diplomatic activities of the... Member States'. In short, Hill argues that EU foreign policy should be understood as the 'sum of what the EU and its Member States do in international relations' (1998, p. 18). In a later article which has 'EU foreign policy' in its title, Hill yet again refers to in the text to European foreign policy as 'the ensemble of the international activities of the European Union, including output from all three of the EU's pillars, and not just that relating to the CFSP' (Hill, 2004, p. 145).

The dilemma whether to choose European foreign policy or EU foreign policy is caused by the confusion of whether the EU possesses a foreign policy and if yes, what does that foreign policy entail. When Keukeleire and MacNaughtan talk about the nature of EU foreign policy in their latest book (2008), they define it in terms of what it is not. As explained, EU foreign policy should not be considered as being equal to CFSP/ESDP (decisions and actions in the former second pillar of the EU), nor to 'European foreign policy' (since the EU does not include all states of Europe and hence 'cannot be equated with "Europe"'), nor to 'the sum of the national foreign policies of EU member states' (p. 29).

EU Foreign Policy and EU External Relations

The above authors agree that a necessary dimension of an EU foreign policy is possessing coherent and strategic actors and institutions. Both Michael and Hazel Smith have pointed out that the EU's first and third pillars of the old EU pillar structure, unlike the second pillar, possessed more coherent institutions (the European Commission) a and strategic set of policies towards third countries (Smith, M., 1998, 2004; Smith, H., 1998) They pointed towards the European Communities and its external relations as the backbone of EU foreign policy.

While external relations may be linked to EU foreign policy, by stretching the boundaries of the concept beyond just the analysis of the CFSP/CSDP, EU's external relations are still not synonymous with EU foreign policy. Keukeleire and MacNaughton have in their most recent book explicitly separated these two terms: 'The difference is not semantic... The vast network of relations the EU has with practically all countries and regions of the world do not alone constitute foreign policy' (2008, p. 199). Unconvinced by the Commission's strategic actorness, they argued that a foreign policy is not just the mere existence and maintenance of these relations but the manner in which the EU strategically uses these relations to pursue its own interests and goals in the respective country or region of the world.

EU Foreign Policy and EU External Action

With the different Treaty reforms and the coming into force of the most recent Lisbon Treaty, the term 'external relations' has in practice and academia been gradually replaced by the term 'external action'. The use of the term 'external action' in the context of the EU can be traced back to the early 2000s and in particular to the period of the European

Convention of 2001–2003 (also called the Convention on the Future of Europe). The Convention included in its activities working groups on different specific subjects, although some of the groups had to have joint meetings on cross-cutting issues. Two groups that had such joint sessions were Working Group VII on External Action and Working Group VIII on Defense. Noteworthy is the choice of the term 'external action' in the name of Working Group VII as well as having a separate working group on defense (Working Group VIII).

In the proceedings of Working Group VII, the relevant documents define EU's external action as a term for all EU actions on the international stage. Chris Patten, European Commissioner for External Relations at the time, emphasized that '"external action" means much more than CFSP... It covers trade, development assistance, humanitarian aid, environment, and issues such as visa and asylum policy *and* foreign policy' (original emphasis, WG VII – WD 29, p. 2). The emphasis on foreign policy being an addition to other EU policies clearly indicates the position that one should not equate foreign policy with external action.

While Chris Patten may have made a distinction between foreign policy and the broader term of external action, this distinction may have been a result of the dominance of the narrow definition of foreign policy of the time within EU circles. However, external action has grown to be synonymous with foreign policy. An illustrating example is the referring to Catherine Ashton, the High Representative of the Union for Foreign Affairs and Security Policy, who is head of the European External Action Service (EEAS), as the 'EU's foreign policy chief' (Moffett, *Reuters*, May 2012).

If one looks at national foreign ministries, the UK, France and Germany being just examples, the competences of these ministries include diplomatic relations, defense issues, asylum and visa issues, development in third world countries and foreign trade, with some of these competencies being shared with the respective ministries of trade, development, internal affairs, etc. The similarity to the EEAS is obvious and comes as no surprise. The EEAS' conceptual predecessor was the envisaged Foreign Ministry of the EU in the Constitutional Treaty. The High Representative of the Union for Foreign Affairs and Security Policy, as she is called today, was named the Union Minister for Foreign Affairs in the final draft of the Constitutional Treaty (Title V).

Considering the increasingly dominant view in the literature that EU's foreign policy should be defined more broadly than just the CFSP/CSDP and include the policies from the former first and third pillars of the EU, as well as considering the fact that such a view is also present in the everyday practice of the EU under the term 'external action', provides sufficient reason to conceptualize EU foreign policy along the lines of EU external action.

Besides a conceptualization, however, analyzing EU foreign policy requires both knowledge of the EU foreign policy decision-making process, the actors involved, a relevant theoretical framework and an analytical model. The following sections will deal with these elements respectively.

The Actors of the Coordinative Discourse in the EU's Foreign Policy

To examine the EU foreign policy process one primarily needs to identify the actual actors involved in the policy-making. At the final stages of the EU foreign policy process, the decisions are made at an intergovernmental forum by democratically elected representatives, namely at the Council of Ministers. However, as some authors have pointed out, the intergovernmental nature of EU foreign policy is fading and is being replaced by a more socialized and integrated, function-oriented EU foreign policy bureaucracy with a common self-identity and purpose (Bickerton, 2011a, b; Tonra & Christiansen, 2004; Vanhoonacker et al., 2010; Howorth, 2000, 2011).

Under such developments the role of the Council is overshadowed by the role of non-elected actors – institutions comprising of seconded officials, diplomats and experts. The main institutions responsible for identifying issues, setting the agenda and framing policy ideas are the Political and Security Committee (PSC), and its advisory bodies: the European Union Military Committee (EUMC) and the Committee for Civilian Aspects of Crisis Management (CIVCOM).

The PSC is '*de facto* the highest administrative body in the ESDP' (Vanhoonacker et al., 2010, p. 9) and performs a number of tasks, from preparing the dossiers related to foreign and security policy for the Committee of Permanent Representatives (COREPER), which then prepares the agenda and dossiers for the Council meetings, to coordinating and supervising the activities of different Council working groups in the area of the CFSP. Another of its responsibilities is the exercise of political control and strategic direction in the case of crisis. In the task of crisis management, the PSC is helped by the Politico-Military Group (consisting of defense counselors and diplomats), the Nicolaidis group, which sets the agenda for the PSC, and the EUMC, which provides recommendation and advice on military matters. The EUMC is the highest military body in the ESDP. It consists of Chiefs of Defense of member states who are often represented by their Military Representatives. The EUMC is assisted by the EUMC working group and the European Union Military Staff (EUMS). The EUMS consists of military and civilian experts seconded by the member states and were integrated in the General Secretariat of the Council but have after the Lisbon Treaty been integrated into the European External Action Service (EEAS).

The CSDP structures responsible for civilian aspects of the policy include the Committee for Civilian Aspects of Crisis Management (CIVCOM) and the Civilian Planning and Conduct Capability (CPCC). CIVCOM consists of representatives from the member states and is in some regards the equivalent of the EUMC, because it gives recommendations and advice to the PSC regarding civilian operations. CIVCOM is assisted by the CPCC, which was integrated in the Council Secretariat and is now part of the EEAS.

Besides the specialized institutions for military and civilian aspects respectively, the CFSP/CSDP benefits from the help of the Crisis Management and Planning Directory (CMPD). The CMPD was created in 2009 and integrated into the EEAS with the purpose of representing a single strategic planning structure in the CSDP.

Besides these institutions, there are other preparatory bodies and actors involved in the early stages of the policy-making process. Working groups consist of members from the Permanent Representations of member states in Brussels and are in charge of drafting and formulating policy. The EEAS and the High Representative of the Union for Foreign Affairs and Security Policy (currently Catherine Ashton) are important actors in coordinating EU's foreign policy both vertically (between member states and the EU level) and horizontally (among institutions). Catherine Ashton and the EEAS have assumed the roles of the former High Representative and the Council Secretariat, which have in the past also proven to be important in the CFSP/CSDP policy process (Dijkstra, 2008, 2010). The EEAS comprises of staff from the Council Secretariat, the Commission as well as seconded officials from member states. Its corporate board and its various managing directorates assist the aforementioned actors with information gathering and processing.

The European Union has also set up three CFSP/CSDP agencies to provide expertise, analyses and information: The European Defense Agency (EDA), the European Union Institute for Security Studies (ISS) and the European Union Satellite Centre (EUSC).

Analyzing EU's Foreign Policy

Possible Approaches

With the concept of EU foreign policy clearly defined and the main actors identified, the next step is to understand how one may study and analyze EU foreign policy as defined above. The two more obvious suggestions are a macro-level, structure oriented view and a micro- or mezzo-level of analysis focusing on agency. The first view proposes to look at EU foreign policy from a macro-level position, as part of a larger structure, which is the world arena. The second view proposes to look at EU foreign policy from a micro- and/or mid-level position, where agency plays a much larger role and to analyze the different actors, institutions and their interactions. Such a view is closer to the subfield of international relation – the field of foreign policy analysis (FPA).

The first view is more concerned with events, developments and the overall impact of EU foreign policy from a macro-level of analysis, while the second view, while not ignoring the outcomes, focuses more on the processes leading up to the outcomes of EU foreign policy. The first view is useful to understand EU's role in the international arena and how this broader structure can influence EU foreign policy, but not necessarily how the EU role is created and changed from within. The second view on the other hand is more analytically rigorous and focuses on agency as the driving force of EU foreign policy development. It focuses on institutions, actors and their relationship to existing structures. However, although the second view may result in a better understanding of the EU and the creation of EU foreign policy, it also poses significantly more problems of operationalisation of foreign policy analysis. The case of EU foreign policy is no different.

Before clarifying the ontological and epistemological standpoints of an FPA approach in the context of EU foreign policy, it is useful to review the existing approaches to FPA. Walter Carlsnaes maps the existing approaches to foreign policy analysis (FPA) in his contribution to the Sage *Handbook of International Relations* (2005, pp. 336–341). The list distinguishes between approaches based on a structural perspective and from an agency-based perspective. Another line of division is drawn between approaches based on a social-institutional perspective and approaches based on an interpretive actor perspective.

FPA approaches based on a structural perspective are closest to and inspired by the discipline and theory of international relations. These approaches include *realist* and *neo-realist* approaches, as well as *neoliberal institutionalism*. Another structure-oriented approach, the *organizational process approach*, borrows from organizational theory and sees organizations as constraining structures on decisions of actors within the organization. Agency-based approaches on the other hand are focusing on a lower level of analysis and the ability of agents to make decisions. Agency-based approaches include *psychological and cognitive approaches* and the *bureaucratic politics approach* (which is similar to the organizational process approach with the difference that agents' decisions are more important than the process itself).

The difference between social-institutional perspective and an interpretive actor perspective is similar to the difference described above, namely between the foci of analysis.

However these two approaches fall into the interpretive epistemological camp. The social–institutional perspective includes *social constructivist approaches* to FPA and *discursive approaches*. These approaches focus on structures of knowledge and their institutional and discursive construction. The interpretive actor perspective aims to focus on the agent and to reconstruct the decision-making process from the perspective of the actor. This perspective also borrows from *role theory* and analyses the role actors play while making decisions. It is clearly an interpretive approach and stresses on subjectivity of perceptions, identities and interests.

While any of the above approaches can be applied to the context of the EU foreign policy, the reality is that there are only few attempts to develop an EU foreign policy analysis model (see White, 2001, 2004a, 2004b; Carlsnaes, 1994, 2005; Waever, 1994, 2001). Brian White (2001) identifies three problems with direct application of what he refers to as traditional FPA to the context of the EU: the inadequacy of the traditional FPA focus on the state; the related need to focus more extensively on what might be called the politics of identity; and the limitations of FPA analysis of the policy process.

The FPA approaches focusing on the state do not explicitly define statehood. These approaches focus on the formal requirements for a state and can be equated with governments. White also criticizes the state-focused FPA approach for equating state with nation and national identity. According to this view, White considers that EU's statehood can be easily challenged due to both lack of a government or a strong collective identity. White therefore suggests that to allow foreign policy analysts to conceptualize the EU as a foreign policy actor, they need to also focus on EU's collective identity formation and points to constructivist literature, in particular to Wendt (1994).

White also points to the potential usefulness of discourse analysis approaches to understanding foreign policy. He refers to Larsen's work and Larsen's critique of mainstream FPA approaches that focus on psychological factors and beliefs. Namely, Larsen argues that these approaches have three main flaws: they focus on the individual decision-maker in foreign policy, they treat beliefs in a positivist manner and finally, they study beliefs and psychological factors relying on the assumption that language is a 'transparent medium' without a dynamic of its own (1997, p. 9).

While White encourages the exploration of discursive approaches to FPA, discursive analysts of EU foreign policy like Larsen and Waever criticize cognitive and psychological approaches and rather stress the importance of identity, norms and ideas as constructed structures that determine policy decisions. Ben Tonra on the other hand encourages cognitive approaches, since they allow one to 'consider ways in which the interests, values, ideas and beliefs of actors are themselves explanatory variables' (2004, p. 8).

This article posits that an agency-oriented yet constructivist and discursive approach to studying EU foreign policy is possible, as well as encouraged. The choice does not have to be either/or; in fact, it may lead to omission in the analysis of crucial variables in explaining EU foreign policy decisions. The next section will first present the theoretical underpinnings of such a model.

The Theoretical Framework

Besides the choices of foci of analysis, the EU foreign policy analyst also requires a theoretical framework for analysis. Although European Union studies have mostly borrowed theoretical concepts and frameworks from the discipline of international relations, EU foreign policy analysts in particular can benefit more from both recent trends in IR theory and institutionalist theories. The recent constructivist turn to international relations has gone a step further in understanding the origins of policies. Instead of taking interests and preferences for granted, the ideas and meanings of the material reality have been taken into account. Discourse theory, a relative of constructivism, can explain how these ideas and meanings are constructed through the use of language. The turn to ideas, interests and change in EU studies originates from the necessity of bridging the existing divide between positivism and constructivism, and between rationalist and ideational explanations of events, especially in institutionalist approaches. An inclusive approach is not only useful, but necessary for the analysis of foreign policy-making and EU's CFSP/CSDP. While material factors inevitably play a great role in explaining policy outcomes, ideas and discourse have considerable explanatory value.

In particular, Teun van Dijk's socio-cognitive approach to discourse analysis (2008) and Vivien Schmidt's discursive institutionalism (2008, 2010) provide for fruitful building blocks of the proposed model for analyzing EU foreign policy. A socio-cognitive approach is necessary to understand the impact of discourses on the construction of meaning and consequently on the cognitive processing of these meanings on an individual and group level. A discursive institutionalist perspective has a great potential for shedding new light on to the complex mechanism of CFSP/CSDP policy-making, and the process of discursive construction within the Brussels-based institutional context. The most elaborate and structured theoretical framework for such an approach is provided by Vivien Schmidt, who is also pushing for the recognition of discursive institutionalism as the fourth 'new institutionalism' (Schmidt, 2010).

Based on these two theoretical frameworks, this article proposes an agency-oriented and institutionalist model of analysis of EU foreign policy. The proposed model is applicable to any institutional setup, including the institutional setup as described above. The model allows insight into the role of actors and their individual contributions to the policy-making process by tracing the process of knowledge and meaning construction through different levels of understanding – exterior to the actors' mind, interior of the actors' mind and a group or organizational level of understanding of reality. Furthermore, the model allows for a stronger role of the agent and for sentient agency, intentionality and individual or group changes to the existing structures.

A Model of Analysis for EU Foreign Policy

Material Reality

The proposed analytical model relies on idealist ontological assumptions, namely that the reality 'out there' cannot exist without our perception and knowledge of it. However, the model does not completely disregard the notion of a material reality. Similarly to the Zen Buddhist koan which asks 'if a tree falls in the forest and there is no one to hear it, does it make a sound', the model deals with the problem of materialistic and idealistic ontological assumptions. A materialistic answer to the koan above would be that the three does make a sound, because it creates sound waves that cut across the air. However, the idealist and constructivist ontological argument would be that the notion of sound is socially constructed by the recipient's perception of those waves, after hitting the eardrum of the recipient.

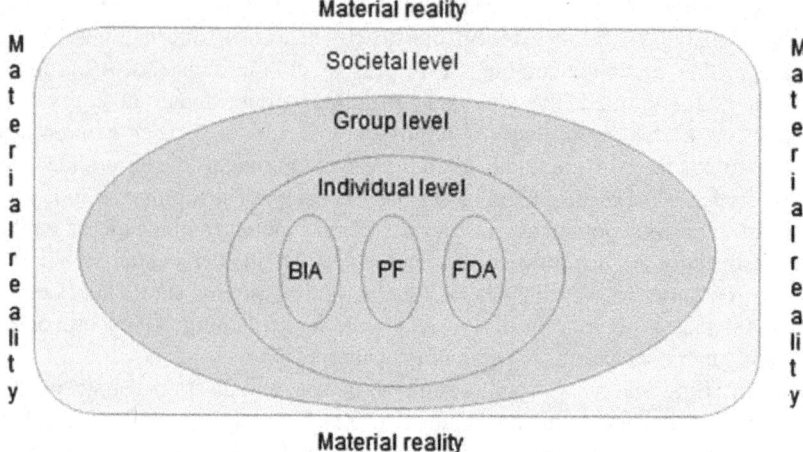

Figure 1. A Model of Analysis for EU Foreign Policy

While the tree may fall without anyone's knowledge of it, its fall only becomes reality after our perception and knowledge of the tree and the fall.

In the case of foreign policy, and in particular, EU foreign policy, the recipients in question are the foreign policy-makers described in the previous section of this article. The reality 'out there' can range from events and situations like wars, political unrests, natural disasters like earthquakes, hurricanes, tsunamis, bush fires to terrorist attacks, pollution or even scientific discoveries. These situations and events are necessary but not sufficient to represent a given reality in the perception of the actors involved in EU foreign policy decision-making. It is also necessary for these actors to be aware of the events and situations out there. In practice this awareness is present due to the established network of both national and Brussels-based intelligence agencies, but also the media, which in a globalized world becomes increasingly important for raising awareness.

However, the knowledge of the events and situations mentioned above is filtered through and by the various levels of recipients. This filtering leads to the epistemological question and assumption of the proposed model. The model relies on a constructivist and interpretivist epistemology. It assumes that the knowledge of the reality 'out there' by the actors involved in EU foreign policy-making is influenced by existing social constructs. The following paragraphs will in more detail explain the cognitive process which is key to the proposed model for analyzing EU foreign policy.

Societal Constructs of Meaning

The social constructs that influence the way actors perceive and conceptualize the world around them can be either constraining or enabling. Constraint in this case refers to the negative influence of socially constructed structures on an absolute objectivity in actors' perceptions of reality. These socially constructed structures include institutions defined in a broader sense and discourses as structures of meaning.

Institutions broadly defined (on a societal level) are social structures that influence individuals' behavior and understandings of their environment. These structures can be patterns of behavior, norms, different types of social rules and beliefs. Examples of institutions can vary from the concept of marriage to religion or, closer to the realm of international relations and foreign policy, to the principles of state sovereignty, international norms, diplomacy or the notion of a nation.

Closely linked to institutions in the broader sense are discourses as structured sets of meanings and carriers of ideas. Discourses are linked with actors' perceptions of reality, and their normative and cognitive ideas of action. Actions (or practice), ideas and norms become institutionalized and are reproduced in a given institutional context. Institutionalist approaches combined with discursive approaches can prove to provide better explanations of the origins and developments of actors' decisions, and in the context of this article, the origins and developments of foreign policies.

One of the proponents of such a combination is Vivien Schmidt and her discursive institutionalism, posited as the 'fourth new institutionalism' (Schmidt, 2008, 2010). Discursive institutionalism is a useful theoretical framework to understand a policy-making process, because it bridges the explanatory gaps of the different strands of institutionalism: rational choice, historical and sociological institutionalism. Discursive institutionalism takes into account both ideas and interests. Its definition of discourse includes both an ideational element (content of discourses) and a dynamic element (process of discursive action). Such a definition of discourse gives more freedom to actors in the structure–agency debate. Although discourses as structures of meaning can constrain actors in their choices of action, they can also enable actors to change the existing structures through the process of discourse (re)creation. The greater focus on agency, enables researches to understand the role of actors and their use of language in the policy-making process.

Linking foreign policy analysis with discourse analysis is a methodologically challenging task. The proposition by Ole Waever posits discourse analysis not just as a methodological and analytical framework for foreign policy analysis, but as a theoretical framework as well, in which the definition of discourse falls towards the structuralist camp. Namely discourse is defined as a structure of meaning, and as Waever argues, 'Structures of meaning can explain and elucidate foreign policy' (Waever, 2001, p. 26). As the argument follows, 'discourses organize knowledge systematically, and thus delimit what can be said and what not' (ibid., p. 29). According to this approach discourse is understood as a precondition to actors' statements. This approach decouples the use of language from the users of language. Instead, language is used when and where appropriate within a given structure of meanings.

Such a structuralist approach to discourse demonstrates weaknesses, because it focuses on the rules of the diffusion of meaning, but not necessarily on the creation of meaning. In other words, it falls back on the typical structure-agency conundrum, favoring the structure side of the debate. The question of where, when, and most importantly, how these structures came into being in the first place, inevitably poses itself. Therefore a more agent-oriented theoretical approach to discourse, like discursive institutionalism as described above can prove more useful in linking discourse analysis with foreign policy analysis. Foreign policy analysis, among other aspects, also focuses on the agent, whether it is a unified actor or a group of actors. In such an approach, discourse is seen as both product and precondition of statements. Discourse, in this view, is the carrier of an ever-changing set of meanings as well as the process in which meanings are reconstructed or preserved.

In foreign policy such an approach is particularly valuable because it allows for analyzing both the content of discourse (the what) as well as the discursive process (the how and the why/when/where/who/to whom). A valuable contribution to the actual method of analysis of discourse in an agent-oriented approach comes from Teun van Dijk and his socio-cognitive approach to discourse analysis (2008). In this approach reality represents subjective experiences of the 'objective', material reality 'out there'. Such an approach posits that the structures of meaning (realities) are created by actors' cognitive processes and reproduced or changed by discursive processes.

It can be equivocal to just say that discourses construct reality. The numerous approaches to discourse however do grant researchers freedom to define in greater length what the phrase 'discourses create reality' means. My take on the question is that discourses construct knowledge, norms and values. Knowledge is simplistically seen as the conception of an individual or society of what is, and includes views and perceptions of reality and feelings and attitudes towards this reality. Norms and values are seen as the conception of individuals or a society of what should be. The existing knowledge and norms represent the 'background ideational abilities' of actors (see Schmidt, 2008, 2010). Focusing away from discourse as only a structure which constrains actors, Schmidt argues that the carriers of discourse are 'sentient agents who construct their ideas conveyed through discourse following a meaning-based logic of communication' (2008, p. 3). Actors use what Schmidt labels as their 'foreground discursive abilities' to react to the constraining structures (institutional and discursive and to change them or at least adapt them to their preference.

The Individual Level: Cognition

The reality 'out there', events and situations, as well as institutions and discourses represent external processes which can generally be considered as context. Context is according to van Dijk (2008) a combination of both spatial–temporal situations (like a terrorist attack or piracy of the coast of Somalia) and social constructs institutions and discourses. The latter represent a layer through which information is filtered before it reaches actors' cognitive process in the brain. Based on the ontological and epistemological assumptions explained above, as well as van Dijk's socio-cognitive approach, the proposed model of analyzing EU's foreign policy posits that contexts are not sufficient to understand the policy-making process. The very term 'process' implies a certain degree of (cognitive) processing. According to the proposed model, the processing (of information from the context) occurs on at least two levels – the individual level and the group level.

The first level is the individual level and occurs in the mind, or in more concrete terms, the brain of the individual. While cognitive psychology still struggles (and may do so in the distant future as well) with understanding how the human brain functions, one can simplify the process and divide it in three steps. The proposed model refers back to Schmidt's notions of 'background ideational abilities' and 'foreground discursive abilities' but complements them with an intermediate stage of the actual preference formation.

The notion of 'background ideational ability' (BIA) invites for some clarification. The term itself seems to imply an ability to have background ideas. While the term may be imprecise, it implies the ability to understand the external processes (events, situations, institutions and discourses) and to manage prior knowledge and experiences by aligning them with the received external impulses. This phase of the cognitive process constantly updates prior knowledge with new external influences, which then becomes new knowledge. This knowledge will become prior knowledge in the next cycle of this mental process.

This step of the cognitive process is also responsible to give meaning to the acquired knowledge. For this, the brain relies on prior meanings, which are socially constructed inter-subjective meanings. The brain also relies on linguistic structures and rules like grammar, semantics and pragmatics.

Both the knowledge acquisition and updating as well the meaning assignment processes constitute what in cognitive psychology is referred to as mental models, or in socio-cognitive approaches like that of van Dijk, as context models (2008). Context models represent the basis of further cognitive processing of the reality 'out there'.

The next step, which the proposed model of this article introduces as an addition to Schmidt's background-foreground model is the phase of preference formation (PF). This phase can be labeled as the 'moment of choice'. Based on the existing prior knowledge and the positions of the knowledge in its respective context model, the individual has the ability of choosing a preferred action (or reaction) in relation to the acquired information and its position in the relevant context models from the previous mental phase.

Introducing this step into the model of analysis enables actors to retain their ability of choice. However, unlike rational choice models, the proposed model stresses the subjectivity of what is understood as 'rationality' in the rational choice models. The choices made by actors are indeed influenced by an array of factors, including external processes and internal processing of those processes. Different (individual) interests, ideas and wants arise at this level depending on individual constellations of prior knowledge and context models. It is at this level that preferences are formed and choices are made.

As a caveat, subjectivity or individuality in the proposed model is conceptualized as a unique, individual constellation of context models. The proposed model does not account for such notions as personality, due to the both conceptual and empirical difficulties this notion creates.

Finally, once the context models have been compiled by the background ideational abilities and based on these context models preferences and choices have been clarified, the actors then can communicate their choices of action (or reaction) by using their 'foreground discursive abilities' (FDA). These abilities entail several communicative, rhetorical and linguistic choices and include choices of words, intonation, ethos and pathos, rhetorical devices, body language, etc. These abilities differ from individual to individual. The levels of persuasion, use of rhetoric and framing and priming abilities constitute the sum of acquired skills, which individuals use to achieve their previously formed preferences through communicative and discursive means.

The Group/Organizational Level

There is however another level of information processing in the EU foreign policy-making process, namely the group level or organizational level. As the different steps at the individual process of cognition, the organizational level has several phases of filtering external processes.

The first step is the individual within a group. The complexities of individuals' information processing are described above. It is however the final of the three internal individual steps that is relevant for the organizational level. The communicative and discursive actions of individuals brought about by their 'foreground discursive abilities' represent the individual contributions to the group's collective or inter-subjective process of social cognition. To avoid terminological confusion, the learning process of a group will henceforth be referred to as the process of organizational learning or group learning, in contrast to an individual's process of cognition.

The nature of interaction between individuals defines the nature of group dynamics. The principles in the discursive activity in the institutional context of CFSP/CSDP in Brussels are consensus, information sharing and coordination. Accordingly, the literature on socialization (Nuttall, 1992, 2000; Lewis, 2005; Manners & Whitman, 2000; Smith, M. E., 2004; Tonra, 2003; Juncos & Pomorska, 2006) will argue that through recurring interaction based on these principles over a longer period of time, the actors in such institutional contexts will develop shared values, beliefs, ideas, and consequentially interests (although not all actors wish to confess to these developments). The peculiarity of the CFSP/CSDP is the interplay between national, member states' interests and the common interest constructed through coordination of national representatives. As described above, increasingly 'national interests are being transformed within a European context' (Tonra, 2000, p. 159).

The individuals' contributions to the group in the form of communicative and discursive action meet the second filter within the group level of processing external processes. This level is the institutional level, with the term 'institution' being narrowly defined. Institutions in the narrow definition differ from institutions defined broadly in the paragraphs above. Institutions in the narrow sense are more similar if not synonymous with organizations. (For a more comprehensive account of the relations between institutions and organizations see Scott, 2007.) Unlike institutions defined more broadly, institutions in the narrow sense are not socially constructed rules of behavior and norms on a broad societal scale. Instead, institutions in the narrow sense are defined as the set of organizational rules of procedure, hierarchies of power, administrative rights and responsibilities, access to information (or intelligence in a foreign policy context), level of clearance, etc.

At this phase of organizational learning the different individual inputs to the policy process are combined with the institutional dynamics in a strictly institutional sense. What is told to whom, how, when and at what level is determined by the institutional formal rules.

There is however a third layer of information processing. The individual inputs are not only confronted with narrowly defined and formal institutional rules, but also with collective institutional informal rules, defined more broadly than the narrow definition in the previous two paragraphs but less broadly understood as the aforementioned socially constructed institutions on a broader, societal level. These institutions are in turn also constructed, but at the level of the organization. The sets of rules, beliefs, norms and worldviews include the organization's set of inter-subjective meanings, its self-image and inter-subjective worldviews. These institutions are common to the organization but may differ from institutions outside of the organization. They may however be shared by other related organizations, which is relevant for the institutional setting of EU foreign policy-making.

Conclusion

The model proposed in the previous section, while complex, is intentionally inclusive of an intermediate organizational level of analysis, which is a necessary level of EU foreign policy analysis. EU foreign policy is created through a layered process within a complex institutional framework, where both organizations and individuals within those organizations share the role of the agent. The proposed model takes into account the different levels of understanding by the relevant policy actors. The model includes both the developments and processes external to the actors' minds, their internal cognitive processes as well as group dynamics and organizational learning processes. Such an inclusive agency-oriented approach provides for a useful tool for tracing the construction and reconstruction of meaning, which both constrains and enables actors to react to a given situation or event.

The model can prove helpful in understanding where certain policies originate from in the first place. With a complex institutional setup, the EU foreign policy poses many difficulties for researchers to understand the different levels of policy-making, the interaction and coordination between the different institutions and finally the origin of policy decisions. The proposed model is applicable to any institution and group of individuals, regardless of their position in the institutional hierarchy.

With the evolving need for efficiency and coherence in EU foreign policy, due to mushrooming of new institutions, understanding the internal dynamics of the respective groups and individual actors represents an important avenue for research. Admittedly, the model requires a micro-level of analysis, which is empirically and methodologically more taxing but may yield more detailed and precise insight into the decision-making process. Furthermore, the conceptualization of EU's foreign policy along the lines of EU external action, as presented in this article, is becoming increasingly prominent in both academia and practice. With the EU increasingly being recognized as an actor that possesses a foreign policy, this model meets the demand of a foreign policy analysis model for the EU context.

Note

[1] The term 'coordinative discourse' refers to Vivian Schmidt's distinction between communicative discourses and coordinative discourses. (Schmidt, 2008, 2010) The latter represents horizontal discursive interactions amongst actors within organizations during policy construction, while the former represents the vertical discursive interaction between these actors and the public. Since the public has little (if any) input in the CFSP and especially in the CSDP policy-making process, the focus on communicative discourse is limited to studies on legitimization of policies, after the policy decisions have already been made. For foreign policy analysts however the interest lies on the process of policy creation prior to decision-making, including the creation of discourses within the policy-making process. Thus, for the purpose of this article and greater clarity, I use the term 'coordinative discourse' when referring to discursive action of EU foreign policy-makers.

References

Bickerton, C. J. (2011a) Towards a social theory of EU foreign and security policy, *JCMS: Journal of Common Market Studies*, 49(1), pp. 171–190.

Bickerton, C. J. (2011b) *European Union Foreign Policy: From effectiveness to functionality* (Basingstoke: Palgrave Macmillan).

Carlsnaes, W. (1994) In Lieu of a Conclusion: Compatibility and the Agency-Structure Issue in Foreign Policy Analysis, in: W. Carlsnaes & S. Smith (Eds) European Foreign Policy: The EC and Changing Perspectives in Europe, pp. 274–87 (London: Sage).

Carlsnaes, W. (2005) Foreign policy. in: W. Carlsnaes, T. Risse & B.A. Simmons (Eds) Handbook of International Relations, pp. 331–49 (Thousand Oaks, CA: Sage Publications).

van Dijk, T. (2008) *Discourse and Context: A sociocognitive approach* (New York: Cambridge University Press).

Dijkstra, H. (2008) The Council Secretariat's role in the common foreign and security Policy, *European Foreign Affairs Review*, 13(2), pp. 149–166.

Dijkstra, H. (2010) Explaining variation in the role of the EU Council Secretariat in first and second pillar policy-making, *Journal of European Public Policy*, 17(4), pp. 527–544.

Hill, C. (1998) Closing the capabilities–expectations gap?, in: J. Peterson & H. Sjursen (Eds) A Common Foreign Policy for Europe? Competing visions of the CFSP, pp. 18-38 (London: Routledge).

Hill, C. (2004) Renationalising or regrouping? EU foreign policy since 11 September 2001, *Journal of Common Market Studies*, 42(1), pp. 143–163.

Howorth, J. (2000) European integration and defence: The ultimate challenge?, *Chaillot Paper 43* (Paris: EUISS).

Howorth, J. (2011) Decision-making in security and defence policy. Towards Supranational intergovernmentalism? *KFG Working Paper Series*, No. 25. Available at http://www.polsoz.fu-berlin.de/en/v/transformeurope/publications/working_paper/WP_25_Howorth.pdf (accessed 20 August 2012).

Juncos, A. & Pomorska, K. (2006) Playing the Brussels game: Strategic socialisation in CFSP Council Working Groups. *European Integration Online Papers (EIoP)*, 10(11). Available at http://eiop.or.at/eiop/index.php/eiop/article/view/2006_011a (accessed 21 August 2011).

Keukeleire, S. & MacNaughtan, J. (2008) *The Foreign Policy of the European Union* (Basingstoke: Palgrave Macmillan).

Larsen, H. (1997) *Foreign Policy and Discourse Analysis: France, Britain, and Europe* (London: Routledge).

Lewis, J. (2005) The Janus Face of Brussels: Socialization and everyday decision-making in the European Union. *International Organization*, 59(4). Available at http://www.journals.cambridge.org/abstract_S0020818305050320 (accessed 26 May 2011).

Manners, I. & Whitman, R. G. (Eds) (2000) *The Foreign Policies of European Union Member States* (Manchester: Manchester University Press).

Moffett, S. (2012) Insight: EU foreign policy chief Ashton stays out of the spotlight. *Reuters*. Available at http://www.reuters.com/article/2012/05/22/us-eu-diplomacy-ashton-idUSBRE84L0ER20120522 (accessed 26 June 2012).

Nuttall, S. (1992) *European Political Co-operation* (Oxford: Oxford University Press).

Nuttall, S. (2000) *European Foreign Policy* (Oxford: Oxford University Press).

Schmidt, V. A. (2008) Discursive institutionalism: The explanatory power of ideas and discourse, *Annual Review of Political Science*, 11(1), pp. 303–326.

Schmidt, V. A. (2010) Taking ideas and discourse seriously: Explaining change through discursive institutionalism as the fourth 'new institutionalism', *European Political Science Review*, 2(1), p. 1.

Scott, W. R. (2007) *Institutions and Organizations: Ideas and interests* (London: Sage).

Smith, H. (1998) Actually existing foreign policy – or not? The EU in Latin and Central America, in: J. Peterson & H. Sjursen (Eds) *A Common Foreign Policy for Europe? Competing visions of the CFSP*, pp. 152–68 (London: Routledge).

Smith, M. E. (2004) *Europe's Foreign and Security Policy: The institutionalization of cooperation* (Cambridge: Cambridge University Press).

Smith, M. H. (1998) Does the flag follow trade? 'Politicisation' and the emergence of a European foreign policy, in: J. Peterson & H. Sjursen (Eds) *A Common Foreign Policy for Europe? Competing visions of the CFSP*, pp. 77–94 (London: Routledge).

Smith, M. H. (2004) Foreign economic policy, in: W. Carlsnaes, H. Sjursen & B. White (Eds) *Contemporary European Foreign Policy*, pp. 75–90 (Thousand Oaks, CA: Sage Publications).

Tonra, B. (2000) Mapping EU foreign policy studies, *Journal of European Public Policy*, 7(1), pp. 163–169.

Tonra, B. (2003) Constructing the CFSP: The utility of a cognitive approach, *JCMS: Journal of Common Market Studies*, 41(4), pp. 731–756.

Tonra, B. & Christiansen, T. (2004) The study of EU foreign policy: Between international relations and European studies, in: B. Tonra & T. Christiansen (Eds) *Rethinking European Union Foreign Policy*, pp. 1–9 (Manchester: Manchester University Press).

Vanhoonacker, S., Dijkstra, H. & Maurer, H. (2010) Understanding the role of bureaucracy in the European security and defence policy: The state of the art, *European Integration Online Papers (EIoP)*, 14(1), Available at http://eiop.or.at/eiop/index.php/eiop/article/view/2010_004a/180 (accessed 2 April 2013).

Waever, O. (1994) Resisting the temptation of post-foreign policy analysis, in: W. Carlsnaes & S. Smith (Eds) *European Foreign Policy: The EC and changing perspectives in Europe*, pp. 238–73 (London: Sage).

Waever, O. (2001) Identity, communities and foreign policy: discourse analysis as foreign policy theory, in: L. Hansen & O. Waever, (Eds) *European Integration and National Identity: The challenge of the Nordic states*, pp. 20–49 (London: Routledge).

Wendt, A. (1994) Collective Identity Formation and the International State, The American Political Science Review, 88(2), pp. 384–96
White, B. (2001) *Understanding European foreign policy* (New York: Palgrave).
White, B. (2004a) Foreign policy analysis and European foreign policy, in: B. Tonra & T. Christiansen (Eds) *Rethinking European Union Foreign Policy*, pp. 45–61 (Manchester: Manchester University Press).
White, B. (2004b) Foreign policy analysis and the new Europe, in: W. Carlsnaes, H. Sjursen & B. White (Eds) *Contemporary European Foreign Policy*, pp. 11–31 (Thousand Oaks, CA: Sage Publications).

The Narrative Construction of the European Union in External Relations

CRISTIAN NIȚOIU
Department of Politics, History and International Relations, Loughborough University, UK

ABSTRACT *The article analyses the way narratives are constructed in EU external relations and their relation to policy practices. Five overarching narratives are identified: the EU as a security provider, the EU as a democratizer and spreader of 'good' norms, the EU as an actor that contributes to or assures global peace, the EU as an entity that contributes to the well-being of peoples around the world and finally the narrative of EU good neighbourliness. After a brief section that details the links between discourses, narratives and political practice, the article will systematically explore the five narratives. The rationale for this endeavour is based on the often huge discrepancy found between the ambitious goals set out in narratives and the poor policy track of the EU in its external relations. Continuous policy and discursive redefinition and reconsideration provide a dynamic context in which goals are renegotiated when political reality deviates from them. A clear pattern of downgrading ambitions when policy outcomes do not match them can be observed in the EU's external relations.*

Introduction

Somewhat decoupled from and antagonistic to the nation state, the European project has spurred the creation of multiple narratives which legitimise its existence. Narratives here are understood to be the product of the overlapping between various discourses which are more fluid and sometimes tend to collide. Only those discourses that are institutionalized through social and political practice come to be part of a narrative. While the nation state is commonly seen as a result or a continuation of the social (Goode, 2005; Fraser, 2007; Linklater, 2007; Nash, 2007) and historical (Deutsch, 1966; Devatak, 1995; Haas, 1958) processes that have affected Europe and the world, the EU resembles more a willingly created political reality to which a number of elites have contributed (Eder, 2007; Fossum & Schlesinger, 2007; Eriksen, 2007). In the case of the nation state narratives are more an expression of a certain social and political reality which is historically constructed. Such narratives tend to reinforce the primacy of the nation state as a centre of power and allegiance. On the other hand, narratives had to be created and distributed throughout the public sphere in order to legitimise the European project as a whole. Either by searching for historical, cultural or social patterns of unity between European peoples, elites (political or intellectual) have sought to frame the Union as a step further in Europe's development. The undeniable economic, social and democratic successes have since the establishment of the Union laid the foundations for the creation of more reality-infused narratives – like with nation states – of economic prosperity, internal peace, tolerance, justice, or respect for human rights that EU had fostered for its member states. Individual citizens and their social imaginaries are continuously addressed through this type of narratives as part of the EU's internal legitimation processes.

A second type of narrative has also been constructed in relations to the EU's self-representation in its external relations. Even less predicated upon the internal successes of the Union, these narratives have focussed on the positive roles the EU can assume in the international system. Chris Bickerton (2011) has highlighted that discourses regarding the foreign policy and external relations of the EU have a functional effect, in that they contribute to the furthering of European integration in situations where internal development seems to be put on halt. To be more clear, narratives regarding the potential that the EU possesses on the international arena have frequently given new meaning and thrust to the European project in times of 'crisis' or deep Euroscepticism. This article maps out the way in which the EU's narratives regarding external relations have impacted on policy outcomes. The rationale for this endeavour is based on the often huge discrepancy found between the ambitious goals set out in narratives and the poor policy track of the EU in its external relations. Continuous policy and discursive redefinition and reconsideration provide a dynamic context in which goals are renegotiated when political reality deviates from them. A clear pattern of downgrading ambitions when policy outcomes do not match them can be observed in the EU's external relations (Bengtsson & Elgström, 2012; Tonra, 2011; Haukkala, 2008). Conversely, the article explores the construction of the EU's external relations narratives in order to understand the above mentioned pattern. Five overarching narratives are identified here: EU as a security provider, EU a democratizer and spreader of 'good' norms, EU as an actor that contributes to or assures global peace, EU as an entity that contributes to the well-being of peoples around the world and finally the narrative of EU good neighbourliness. After a brief section that details the links between discourses, narratives and political practice, the article will go on to systematically explore the five narratives.

Discourses and Narratives

Discourse can be considered to have different facets and qualities. It is both the process and the background through which ideas and social practices become created, institutionalized and reified. Discourse goes beyond the text which expresses it, highlighting social and communicative practices that contribute to the construction of group identities (Stråth & Wodak, 2009, p. 28). Through overarching common narratives, discourses can transcend social and political borders and shape social imaginaries beyond those that gave birth to them. There is also an imbedded sense of historicity in the construction of discourses (Krzyżanowski et al., 2009, p.6). Europe's different meanings and its continuous negation with the nation state are seen here as parts of a wider historical process where discourse drives forward social and political change but also has the ability to institutionalize a certain *status quo*. For this reason the more or less wilful reproduction of discourses can lead to 'rhetorical entrapments', whereby actors are constrained to accept the practical outcomes of their prior acceptance of certain discourses although these might not match current the social or political reality. Conversely, an analysis of discourse can shed light on why certain ideas come to have significant power in shaping social practices and political practices. However, such an approach implies an intrinsic difficulty as discourses although historically constructed tend to be fluid and rather impossible to pin down, but at the same time difficult to overlook: 'neither absolute fixity nor absolute non-fixity is possible' (Laclau & Mouffe, 2001, p. 111).

On the other hand, narratives are the result between the overlapping of various discourses which can provide a much clearer picture of the processes behind the creation of ideas and their influence on political and social reality. In instances when they become shared by a broader political community, narratives tend to be 'liberated' from the dynamism that characterizes discourse. Only those discourses that are institutionalized and enacted have the potential to create such widely shared narratives. Consequently narratives, regarding 'Europe' or the 'EU' – which address mostly its citizens or public sphere(s) – do not have a coherent essence and are at the intersection of various discourses. Gerard Delanty and Chris Rumford (2005, p. 20) have identified a cosmopolitan narrative of the EU which frames it as an entity that transcends different political and discursive borders. It has at its roots various social, economic and political achievements of the European Union, and plays a functional role in creating what Fuchs (2011) calls ontological support which is not dependent on future policy successes but relies on a shared common memory and feeling of effectiveness. Discourses are here are created by a shared inter-subjective social imaginary. Europeaness is situated at the intersection between popular day-to-day experiences in 'Europe' and the understandings that political elites have of them. Both top-down and bottom-up processes are at work although one cannot overlook the increasing popularity the elite constructed idea of EU exceptionalism is having. Tonra (2011, p. 1192) highlights that 'policy elites have assiduously developed narratives of European exceptionalism as if to underpin their own self understanding of the unique political project that they have undertaken', narratives which seem to have been also adopted by European citizens.

V. A. Schmidt (2008) has distinguished between two types of discourses within a political community which intersect and give birth to narratives. Coordinative discourses describe practices that take place within political institutions far from the public eye and are most times aimed at gaining social support from the actors who possess political knowledge and power. The public is addressed through communicative discourse which seeks to convince individuals regarding the necessity of different policy approaches. Both these types of communication play their part in the construction of the European Union's narratives in external relations, although coordinative ones are considered to have a more central role (Manners, 2010; Tonra & Christiansen, 2005; Zielonka, 2007). However, the EU's narratives in its external relations seem to have been highly stable and rather cumulative since the Union's creation, making it all the more difficult to draw a clear distinction between the ideas promoted by communicative and coordinative discourse. Such narratives, even more than ones referring to the internal ontology of the EU have been contingent upon 'path dependency' processes within institutions and 'rhetorical entrapments' at all levels within society. Their construction has been much more top-down and characterized by a snowballing effect where shared narratives created in the past are continuously accrued with new institutionalized discourses. Nonetheless, the same process cannot be observed when one explores the practical effects of the narratives. Political outcomes in external relations are, of course, subject to many more external constraints besides the narratives that inform their goals. This makes it even more legitimate to map out the way the EU's narratives in external relations affect its policy outcomes.

In the particular case of the European Union, and especially its external relations one more type of discourse which is also integral to the EU's narratives has to be discussed. Scholarly discourse regarding the external relations of the EU has an important role in the construction of such narratives. Most scholars tend to share an underlying optimism towards potential of the European Union to play an important role in international system (Tonra, 2011, p. 1192). A similar observation was made in the past in relation to realism as being an American social science whose only role was to legitimate and inform the foreign policy of the US (Hoffmann, 1977). However, in EU external relations scholarship there seems to be a higher degree of diversity than there was at that time in IR theory. To be short, Robert Cox's (1981) famous notion of the problem solving theory is irrelevant when applied to the case of the EU, as scholars both criticise and propose solutions for strengthening the Union's role in the international system. Nonetheless, contributions tend to converge around more or less obvious support and optimism towards the potential of the EU on the international arena. The remainder of article will analyse the way in which the types of discourses highlighted above overlap and create five narratives of the EU in external relations. A special attention will be afforded to the way elites have framed the narratives both in official documents and statements. According to Entman (1993, p. 152) framing means 'to select some aspects of a perceived reality and make them more salient in a communicating text, in such a way as to promote a particular problem definition, causal interpretation, moral evaluation, and/or treatment recommendation'. Identifying the linkages between discourses within the five narratives will facilitate mapping out the latter's influence on policy outcomes in EU external relations.

The EU as a Promoter of Peace

The official narrative regarding the Union's ability to foster global peace has been built on the peaceful experience of the European continent during the last 60 years. Overcoming the scourge of war and the hazardous national interests and tendencies that often led to it, Europe is presented having developed a new mode of Kantian interaction between its member states. The European Union has thus a duty to share the lessons learned in maintaining peace on the continent and convince other states to relinquish behaviours that could lead to confrontation or war. This idea of a somewhat 'sacred' duty is best summarized by European Commission president Barosso (President of the European Commission, 2005): 'having stumbled across such a successful formula for spreading peace and stability on our own continent, it is only natural to offer our know-how and experience to encourage peace and stability elsewhere in the world'. Articulated in such terms the narrative of the EU as a promoter of global peace seems to have rather a unilateral logic, where the Union promotes a certain set of solutions without fully considering the particularities of the countries or regions in question. However, in recent years Lady Ashton has discursively acknowledged the need for the Union to consider a qualitative change in how it 'approaches the challenges of pursuing peace by guaranteeing that the basic rights and needs'[1] of individuals around the world.

The practical failures of the Union's approaches to global peace and stability have been often been explained at the official level by alluding to the reluctance of domestic actors in undemocratic countries to fully adopt the EU's proposed reform. For example, in relation to the conflict in Somalia, Lady Ashton has been firm in arguing that the EU cannot move forward in promoting peace in the region while necessary reforms are being ignored by authorities and warlords.[2] The continuous redefinition of approaches to global peace together with the European 'blame-game' fit well into to the overarching pattern identified in the Union's behaviour. Conversely, when the Union's efforts directed at promoting global peace fall short of its ambitious goals, the EU downgrades its expectations in order to match policy outcomes. Even more, a 2010 European Parliament standard briefing 'Towards an EU peacebuilding strategy?' suggests that the EU's deficiencies in promoting peace lay mostly in the amount of resources mainstreamed in this direction, and the lack of political will from member states. Better coordination with the United Nations' efforts which has significantly more experience in fostering strategic and on the ground long-term peace is perceived as paramount for the success of the EU. The briefing also identifies that the EU's ambitious rhetorical strategy is not backed up by practical achievements due to the existing fragmentation which is undesirable in terms of 'coherence, effectiveness, and clarity towards donor countries, but also with regard to democratic legitimacy, speed of implementation, and decision-making' (European Parliament, 2010, p. 7).

Diez (2005) has argued that the construction of the narrative of Europe as a promoter of global peace is part of the larger self-image of the EU as a normative power. The normative discourse is used in the case of the EU as a way of distinguishing it from the other. The EU positions itself as a unique international actor that has its main goal and duty in promoting its peace for the emancipation of other states and peoples. Immediately such rhetoric encompasses the idea that other states are inferior in their foreign policy, because unlike the EU they do not share this goal of promoting universal norms and trying to act as emancipatory powers. This move is legitimized by the idea that the EU went through a massive normative transformation. If before the Second World War, Europe was a continent plagued with wars and conflicts, after 1945 the EU managed to create a new discourse and identity based on solidarity between its states and nations, and on the peace and respect for democracy and human rights. The past of the EU becomes the absolute other in the construction of the normative Europe narrative – *the past as other* (Diez, 2005, p. 634). Consequently, all non-EU states are judged according to the past image of Europe and in most cases – the US, or Australia or Canada seem not to fit within this discourse – they are deemed to behave similarly or even less normative. As such, the EU has a duty to promote – even impose – its norms in the states who still act as Europe did before 1945 (Cooper, 2007).

In scholarship the well-known dissonance between the Union's capabilities and expectations or more recently aspirations has been considered to be the prime factor responsible for the lack of effectiveness in the EU's approach to global peace. Hill (1993, p. 322) proposed almost two decades ago that the EU could surmount this gap by lowering its expectations and standards in order to match the policy instruments and resources that are available to it. More recently, Smith (2011) has underscored that the capabilities–expectations gap should be better seen as a capabilities-aspiration gap as the ambitious goals of the Union seem to have increased sharply since Hill first recognised the gap. In this case, prioritization of goals becomes the only suitable strategy if the EU is to implement effectively any of its aspirations. Smith's proposals collides with the actual practice of the EU, which seems to prioritize its rhetoric in relation to policy outcomes, overlooking the important question whether it possesses instruments to pursue any of its discursively (re)framed aspirations. Due to this, in crisis situations the European Union was unable to act building on its own resources, having to fall back on the instruments of the member states. For example, the evacuations of European officials from Libya and the involvement of member states were fully delivered through national involvement (Tonra, 2011, p. 1201). However, the ever rising aspirations of the Union can be linked to the views expressed by citizens arguing for a stronger European foreign policy that can effectively deliver global peace and stability.[3] This adds internal legitimacy to the narrative of the promotion of global peace, even though policy outcomes tend to fall short of the EU's ambitious goals.

The Democratization Narrative

Within the EU democracy is considered to be predicated upon two other aspects: communication and multilevel governance. According to the White Paper on a European communication policy (European Commission, 2006, p. 6) democracy cannot be achieved without building a communicative link with citizens. This involves promoting three broad principles: *inclusiveness* – political language should be accessible to all strata of society; communication practices should be *diverse* and address and take into account equally all the views expressed in public debate; finally, citizens should have the opportunity to express their views and *participate* in political practices. The application of these principles would not only connect citizens to national or European institutions but would promote the right to information and freedom of speech. On the other hand, the White Paper on European governance – 'Enhancing democracy in the European Union' – highlights the second crucial aspect of European democracy, that of the considerable number of checks that multilevel governance puts on decision making processes in the EU, making them more democratic (European Commission, 2000, p. 5).

However, Fuchs (2011) has pointed out that the transfer of sovereignty which gave birth to the Union was not accompanied by an increase in transparency and accountability, creating a deep democratic legitimacy crisis which is yet to have been mitigated through coherent policies and initiatives by the EU. The Union's internal democratic issues have also spilled over into the way it promotes democracy in other states. According to Biscop (2010, p. 76), the Union has been willing to sacrifice the promotion of civil rights and liberties in the ENP states in favour of the assurance of political stability that could secure the EU economic interests. Nonetheless, most scholarship on EU external relations would agree that 'democracy is thought not to mix well with foreign policy' (Chris Patten quoted in Bickerton, 2011, p. 101) making it hard both to promote democracy 'all the way', or to do this in a democratic manner. An approach focused on incremental steps that can build or encourage both bottom-up and top-down democracy building initiatives is widely acknowledged as the most appropriate for the EU (Kantner & Liberatore, 2006; Youngs, 2010; Wolf, 1999; Christou, 2010; Manners, 2010).

Official narratives regarding the EU's external promotion of democracy tend to overlook the internal democratic crisis that the Union faces. For example, the High Representative of the Union for Foreign Affairs and Security Policy, Lady Ashton has been central in advocating a new European approach to democracy that seemingly has a more profound influence not only on political systems but also on political cultures. The European Union has not been quite successful in fostering for prolonged periods sustainable democratic practices in its Eastern neighbourhood (Averre, 2009). Conversely, the move envisaged by Ashton would imply tackling political issues at their roots, because only in this way could 'true democracy'[4] be developed. Europe is identified here to be effective in dealing and encouraging civil society and securing individual rights and liberties through police missions. Even European Commission president Barosso[5] underscored the Union's commitment to endorse additional funding for the reforms in European countries in order to promote 'deep democracy'. This has happened because, as Ashton (2011) puts it:

> ... democracy is, of course, about votes and elections – but it is also about far more than that. What we in Europe have learned the hard way is that we need 'deep democracy': respect for the rule of law, freedom of speech, an independent judiciary and impartial administration. It requires enforceable property rights and free trade unions. It is not just about changing government but about building the right institutions and attitudes. In the long run, 'surface democracy' – people casting their votes freely on election day and choosing their government – will not survive if deep democracy fails to take root.

Both the ambiguity and indecisiveness of scholarly discourse which seems only to legitimate official rhetoric and the ever shifting goals of the EU in terms of democracy have created a great discrepancy between the narrative of democratisation and policy outcomes. Three main reasons can account for this. Firstly, the European Union seems to be unwilling to back its ambitious rhetoric with political commitment. A large discrepancy arises between the normative/idealistic Union's discourse and its practical policy outcomes, which in the end hinders the paths towards democracy of the countries in question. The EU is conscious of its poor practical policy record caused by the lack of political will, and always tries to adapt its discourse to the realities on the ground. Benchmarks defining what a successful policy means get downgraded in order to match the European Union's poor outcomes in promoting democratisation. Secondly, the EU applies an asymmetric approach to its relations with third party states which hinges upon the a priori acceptance of its conditionality. Coupled with the lack of political will that characterizes the Union, the promotion of human rights and other such norms becomes torn apart between the democratic ideal and a tendency to promote regional stability. Nonetheless, Youngs (2010) highlights that at the local level EU diplomats strive to advance processes of democratisation but most often these efforts are not complemented by the member states or even Brussels. Finally, what this points to is an overarching reluctance on the part of the European Union to meaningfully back up its ambitious discourse in third party states.

Good Neighborliness

The narrative that portrays the Union as a good neighbor is based on the belief that the EU should build or is striving to build a partnership with its neighbors, through which it could spread a series of universal norms and values. According to Agh (2010, p. 1240), the success of the EU in its neighbourhood is paramount for proving the ability of the Union to act in a normative or civilian manner on a global scale. External sources of legitimacy are required in order for the EU to advance its set of normative narratives (Manners, 2010, p. 38). Officially, the ENP is built on the assumption that states from the EU's neighbourhood have to comply to or make good use of the help the Union provides. Cooperation between the EU and its neighbours increases only if the latter adapt to the Union's requirements and incorporate its advice 'chapter by chapter in a very well-organized fashion'.[6] A more cosmopolitan and less unilateral approach has been recently publicized by Lady Ashton. In her view the ENP is more than a tool for integrating the Union's neighbours; it functions more as a partnership where the EU has also a lot to benefit from. Conversely, the Union's efforts are aimed towards 'the people striving for democracy, freedom, and a better life'.[7] Defined as such, the ENP seems to employ the same mechanism of conditionality like those at play in the last enlargement towards Central and Eastern Europe. The Union has been quite clear in removing any promise or hint of future membership for the countries from its neighbourhood, although it has never entirely rejected the prospect. The official narrative acknowledges the mutual benefits that enhanced cooperation with the EU's neighbours can have, but highlights that membership cannot add value to both parties and their relationship:

> But being closer to the European Union doesn't mean being part of the European Union. And of course we can sign with countries very profound cooperation agreements, but membership is a different story that cannot be infinite in number, you have to understand that. We never say, 'No', but we say let's keep on moving and let's keep on cooperating as much as possible.[8]

Both theoretically and practically the ENP, at least in its eastern concerns, isn't as complete or stable as officials in the Commission portray it. Christou (2010, p. 148) has posited that the ENP is the result of a double narrative which is detrimental to the development of a sustainable security environment in the region, and of the economies of the eastern neighbours of the EU or their citizens' welfare. On the one hand, the EU portrays itself as a *force for good* that promotes its norms for the well-being of other peoples. However, it was underlined above that there are various contradictions which plague the Union's normative approach and have the potential of determining its failure. On the other hand, another hidden and more malign narrative can be identified in the EU's policy in the eastern neighbourhood. Asymmetrical bilateral relations are the primary mode of interaction preferred by the European Union in the ENP. Europe's norms – be they democratic or liberal – gain pre-eminence over the culture and the values of the *other*.

Like in the case of the other narratives explored in this article, effective and successful policy outcomes are considered evidence of the existence of a coherent European Union foreign policy (Ashton, 2011). The 2008 conclusions of the Council regarding the European Neighborhood Policy underscored the effectiveness of the ENP as a tool for promoting reform in the EU's neighbors. The ENP was identified to have fostered sectoral reform and modernization through the action plans, and has also implemented a series of benchmarks regarding human rights, democracy or rule of law (Council of the European Union, 2008). In the autumn of 2011 the member states reiterated the fact that 'the Eastern Partnership is based on a community of values and principles of liberty, democracy, respect for human rights and fundamental freedoms, and the rule of law' (Council of the European

Union, 2011, p. 2). The summit also recognized the need to increase the sense of ownership of the ENP within the countries in the region. Considerable progress was also acknowledged to have been achieved towards building multilateral platforms where the Union would interact on equal terms with its Eastern neighbors.

The pattern of downgrading goals in order to match policy outcomes is ever present with the narrative of good neighbourliness. As the core motivation behind the ENP is the need to extend the control of the EU beyond its borders (Tonra, 2010, p. 66), the Union is always willing to sacrifice its aspirations in the region in order to achieve stability and safeguard its economic interests. While the official discourse defines a series of ambitious goals, practice points to the tendency of the European Union to prefer regional or domestic stability over reform in ENP countries. Conversely, when the EU speaks of human security in ENP a dilemma between democracy and stability arises (Biscop, 2010, p. 77). For example, in its relations with Eastern neighbours the Union's weak presence and efforts shaped by a deep lack of political willingness have attracted considerable criticism. Wolczuk (2010, p. 48) contends that due to the overriding interests of Russia in the region the EU chooses to promote an abstract notion of good governance which obscures directly engaging the peaceful resolution of frozen conflicts.

Official discourse also underscores that the European Union seeks to promote three Ms in its relations with its neighbours: mobility for educational and business purposes; money for the assurance of sustainable development through project financed by the Union; and the market; symbolized by the need to integrate the markets in the EU's neighbourhood and to enable the free flow of capital and goods (European Commission High Representative, 2011b). One should not overlook the traction that the EU's discourses have had since the creation of the ENP in the countries in the region. Rational choice theory might provide a satisfactory explanation for why the leaders of the ENP countries choose to follow a European path due to the potential of considerable economic gains, but it cannot account for the 'discursive power of arguing, framing, and attaching meaning to a set of ambiguous concepts, such as democracy, human rights, and good governance—indeed, attempting to shape conceptions of "normality"' (Bengtsson & Elgström, 2012, p. 101). This is why even when the Union falls short of strongly engaging with the issues in its neighborhood, continuously downgrading its aspirations, the narrative of good neighborliness continues to be perceived as legitimated by states at the Union's borders.

The Security Narrative

A central aspect of the official discourse of the EU regarding its ability to provide security is the idea that political development is highly dependent on the assurance of security, as conflicts or criminality tend to hamper sustainable economic growth and the spread of democracy. The 2003 European Security Strategy 'A secure Europe in a better world' (Council of the European Union, 2003, pp. 4–5) identified five key global threats: terrorism, the proliferations of weapons of mass destruction, regional conflicts, state failure and organized crime. Besides these, energy security was framed as a special concern for Europe due to its high level of imports from unstable and in some situations undemocratic countries. According to the document, each of these challenges due to their diverse nature had to be tackled through a mixture of instruments, mechanisms and strategies. Smith (2011, p. 146) contends that while the EU's discourse regarding the redefinition of global threats to security has been both innovative and partially put into practice, it has failed because it has not created a wide platform of joint action between the member states based on the principles of solidarity and burden sharing.

The European Union has made the concept of solidarity one of its central guiding principles. However, when it comes to energy security or Europe's security relations with Russia, division rather than solidarity characterize the Union's approach. Member states seem to be more prone to develop enhanced bilateral relation with Russia than achieve a common united stance. These enhanced relations have been characterized by strong economic and energy security ties modelled on the approaches of big EU players like Germany or France. For example, Germany became, during Putin's leadership, Russia's most important trade partner and a close supporter of its energy policy. Moscow has also made use of differentiated energy prices, and gas and oil embargoes to project its hard power, while the EU has only managed to impose travel bans in cases where ENP countries were steering in the wrong direction (Cichocki, 2010; Biscop, 2010). European official have on the other hand avoided the question of solidarity in energy security, and at times have overtly affirmed its practical manifestation suggesting the effort to diversify oil and gas supply as evidence for this:

> We take this concept of solidarity extremely seriously, as we have shown during the most recent Russia–Ukraine gas crisis. We are now taking structural action at the European Union level for energy security and energy diversification. (President of the European Commission, 2010)

In practice, the security narrative has come to be equated only with civil operations and tackling non-traditional security threats due to the failure of the EU to live up to its plans of building strong and flexible military capabilities. Such approaches centred on member states have overlooked the influence of domestic factors such as the views and interests of the public. In his account of the influence of public opinion on the creation of a military force, Wagner (2007, p. 2) argued that the goal of creating an European military force increases the pressures on the member states to contribute financially to a policy which in most cases isn't supported by their citizens. Data from the Eurobarometre confirms his views and shows that most European citizens do not favour an EU that spends massively to support military operations throughout the world. Additionally, EU citizens hugely support a foreign policy of the EU that is bent on promoting its norms and values but that it is done without financial involvement (European Commission, 2010b). However, decisions in the field of security in the EU are most times taken with working groups and shrouded by mystery. This renders public access virtually impossible and at most restrictive, decreasing the transparency and accountability of polices adopted in the field of security (Juncos & Pomorska, 2011, p. 1110).

Leaving aside the discrepancy between the EU's ambitious discourses and its policy outcomes, the security narrative distinguishes itself from the other four by the fact that goals tend to remain constant and are not downgraded in order to match practical consequences of policies. It is more that policy failures and realities are overlooked, while aspirations are continuously backed and restated. The 2008 *Report on the Implementation of the European Security Strategy* (Council of the European Union, 2008b, p. 1) reassured that the EU was on track in tackling the challenges identified five years before. It finds that the Union has acted as an anchor of stability, providing security both in its neighborhood and globally. Strengthening institutional capabilities in order for them to deliver strategic diplomacy and decision making was considered here to be one of the areas were considerable work still needed to be done. Secondly, the document mentioned the need for the continuous development of military capabilities coupled with burden sharing-initiatives between the member states that could facilitate the EU to 'be force for a fairer, safer and more united world' (Council of the European Union, 2008b, p. 10). Within the ever changing international context the Union had be more present in shaping global events, for only such a strategy could build a 'secure Europe in a better world' (Council of the European Union, 2008b, p. 12). Conversely, on more than one occasion Lady Ashton has articulated the idea that the EU should assume a position of global responsibility due to the increasing demand for the EU to engage more forcefully in providing global security. At the same time, the EU should try to promote solutions that are efficient both in terms of policy outcomes and funding. However, the official discourse, as in the case of the narratives that presents the EU as fostering democracy around the world, seems to favour measures that focus on 'underdevelopment, weak institutions and lack of democracy and respect for human rights' (European Commission High Representative, 2011a), rather than on those that imply a direct engagement with the challenges identified by the European Security Strategy.

EU and the Well-being of Peoples around the World

Climate change and development policy seem to be the only policy areas in external relations where officially EU elites have recognized the need to match the ambitious rhetoric with practical outcomes. Barosso was keen to highlight that 'it is clear to us that our current ambitious policy is working; but now it needs to be backed up over the long term'.[9] The European Union has also committed itself to tackling the consequences of natural or manmade disasters which can result in 'loss of human lives and property, including cultural heritage, the destruction of economic and social infrastructure and damage to the environment' (Council of the European Union, 2007, p. 1). Even more than this, the EU has sought to develop a series of instruments through which it could pressure other states to drive forward a progressive agreement on global climate change policy and foster an integral approach to development aid that could be adopted by all major donors. Nonetheless, recent events in the international system – like the failure of the 2009 Copenhagen summit – have underscored the fact the while the EU might promote a series of normative aspirations and in some case might also back them up with political willingness, other powerful actors are still driven by a self-interested narrow logic (Cooper, 2007). Recognizing this situation Lady Ashton has mentioned on several occasions the need to promote global collaboration and convince other important global actors to cooperate:

> Collaboration means we use our economies of scale, the ability to deliver for each other in different parts of the world where we are more active, the capacity to think together about how to make the most difference in the least possible time to support people who are trying to grapple with some fundamental issues of development.[10]

Climate change has been framed in official discourse as a threat to the well-being of peoples around the world due to its potential hazardous economic and social impact on regions which are already impoverished and in a disadvantaged structural position

(European Commission, 2009, p. 4). The EU has framed itself as a leader in global climate change policy due to the multitude of instruments tools at its disposal and its commitment to multilateralism. According to former High Representative Javier Solana the EU saw itself 'as 'catalyser' in a global search for a deal on climate change'[11] that would aid developing states and would lead to the implementation of ambitious policies. If the EU is to achieve this role, climate change measures within the Union would have to be taken at all levels: regional national and local in order for the EU to present itself as a model of adopting ambitious and progressive policies for tackling climate change.

A recent defining moment can be considered here to be the climate Conference in Copenhagen in December 2009, where the EU expressed a huge sense of disappointment after a constructive international accord could not be reached. The Union has always showed itself to be a supporter of the UN process on climate change and has set in this matter ambitious goals both domestically and globally. The official narrative of the failure puts the blame on other world powers like the US or China for their unwillingness to make any environmental concessions. The Union's perceived failure in Denmark also had the effect of undermining its assumed normative global leadership on climate change. Official reports from the Commission (2008, 2010) on the post-Copenhagen climate outlook have underlined that the failure in Denmark has made developing countries more mistrustful. In turn, this can only be mitigated if the EU increases its global legitimacy by employing more drastic domestic environmental policies.

One cannot overlook the fact, that Europe's narrative of promoting the well-being of peoples all around the world has been constructed in relation and in opposition to the action of the United States. Issues of international development and climate change have been the important points of divergence in EU–US relations over the past years. The most important derives from different approaches that the two actors have towards multilateralism. The EU seems to be more open to engage in multilateralism than the United States. In the case of climate change, a second aspect that has caused rifts between the Union and its transatlantic counterpart is related to the fact that, up until the Copenhagen summit, the EU was considered to be an undisputed global leader in climate change policy. At the same time, it should be noted that many politicians and analysts from the US still regard climate change or international development as a matter of low politics, secondary to hard issues in international politics – which might help account for the EU's almost two decades of continuous leadership (Falkner, 2007; Harris, 2007; Kelemen, 2010; Kelemen & Vogel, 2009). In a realist interpretation of these events, Paterson (2009, p. 145) has suggested that EU–US relations in climate change are characterized by hegemonic rivalry where one actor rejects cooperation and seeks to thwart the other's superior position. As such, both actors have sought to adapt to the leadership claims of the other, possibly causing prolonged conflict. From the EU's perspective, it has tried to engage the US to adopt the same strict domestic regulations in order for its firms not to lose in terms of competitiveness to the American ones. The European Union has been frequently overt in criticizing the US for not ratifying the Kyoto treaty and not taking climate seriously (J. R. Schmidt, 2008, p. 92). Conversely, the narrative of the EU's ability to promote and secure the well-being of peoples around the world has not been subject to the same trend of downgrading goals in order to reflect practical policy outcomes. It is more that failures have been legitimated by identifying scapegoats – like the US or China – who are unwilling to cooperate and adopt the high global standards proposed by the EU.

Conclusions

This article has explored the overlapping between various discourses in EU external relations, in order to highlight the way in which narratives are constructed. While discourses are considered to be fluid, continuously interacting with each other, narratives are constructed only by those discourses that become institutionalized through political and social practice. Moreover, narratives regarding the EU's external relations tend to be cumulative in the sense that new institutionalised discourses have the power to modify or replace altogether earlier ones. This process can be observed in relation to three of the narratives identified in the article. Goals and aspiration are continuously reconsidered (most times downgraded) in order to match policy outcomes and political reality. Through this the EU's external relations are provided a justification, for the success and effectiveness of practical policies is widely acknowledged at the official level as a trade mark of a coherent and well coordinated European foreign policy.

Within the last 20 years aspirations in the EU's external relations seem to have increased sharply, partly based on the overwhelming popular preference for more *Europe* in foreign policy. Policy outcomes, on the hand, have been poor and have not lived up to the ambitious goals on which the five narratives identified in the article are predicated on. Two other strategies besides the continuous reconsideration of goals were employed at the official level for legitimising the EU's efforts in external relations. In the case of the security narrative, reality has been manufactured in the process of overlooking practical policy failures. Secondly, the narrative that portrays the EU as contributing to the well-being of peoples around the world has blamed the US, China, Russia and other emerging countries for not adopting the Union's normative approach and hampering its global endeavours. Nonetheless, it must be noted that the creation of the European External Action Service has marked a slight tendency of trying to find a balance between rhetoric and political practice which can bring a higher degree of coherence and effectiveness in the EU's external relations. But the discrepancy between narratives and policy outcomes will not be mitigated unless the Union does not manage to extract political willingness from the member states and develop both its power resources and foreign policy instruments.

Notes

[1] EU's Ashton makes fresh push to revive peace talks. *EUbusiness* [online], 24 January 2012. Available at http://www.eubusiness.com/news-eu/israel-palestinians.er8 (accessed 10 February 2012).

[2] Ashton condemns Somalia bombing: reaffirms support for peace. *New Europe* [online], 5 October 2012. Available at http://www.neurope.eu/article/ashton-condemns-somalia-bombing-reaffirms-support-peace (accessed 10 February 2012).

[3] During recent years opinion polls have recorded Europeans being in favour of a Europe that is more engaged in global affairs: for example a 2006 Eurobarometre (European Commission, 2007) shows that around 80% of the European citizens support more EU involvement in the global fight against terrorism or the spread of peace and democracy around the world.

[4] Ashton has frequently defined European democracy as the true democracy for it lays the foundations for peace, prosperity and tolerance. For example: EU'S Ashton campaigns for 'deep democracy. *Reuters* [online], 13 November 2011. Available at http://www.reuters.com/article/2011/11/13/us-eu-forpol-libya-idUS-TRE7AC0WX20111113 (accessed 10 February 2012).

[5] Barroso pledges €1.24 billion for EU's neighbours. *European Voice* [online], 24 May 2011. Available from: http://www.europeanvoice.com/article/2011/may/barroso-pledges-1-24-billion-for-eu-s-neighbours/71158.aspx (accessed 10 February 2012).

[6] Former High Representative for Foreign and Security Policy, Javier Solana in: 'EU: Solana says membership for Caucasus "A different story"'. *Radio Free Europe/Radio Liberty* [online], 15 November 2006. Available at http://www.rferl.org/content/article/1072738.html (accessed 10 February 2012).

[7] Lady Asthon in: 'EU pledges more funding as it unveils revamped neighborhood policy'. *Radio Free Europe/Radio Liberty* [online], 25 May 2011. Available at http://www.rferl.org/content/eu_pledges_funding_unveils_-revamped_neighborhood_policy/24196916.html (accessed 10 February 2012).

[8] Former High Representative for Foreign and Security Policy, Javier Solana in: 'EU: Solana says membership for Caucasus "A different story"'. *Radio Free Europe/Radio Liberty* [online], 15 November 2006. Available at http://www.rferl.org/content/article/1072738.html (accessed 10 February 2012).

[9] 'EU climate chiefs in row over future of emissions trading'. *The Guardian* [online], 17 June 2011. Available at http://www.guardian.co.uk/environment/2011/jun/17/european-energy-emissions-trading-row (accessed on 10 February 2012).

[10] Ashton: 'EU needs "creative" relations with BRICS'. *Public Service Europe* [online], 8 February 2012. Available at http://www.publicserviceeurope.com/article/1475/ashton-eu-needs-creative-relations-with-brics (accessed 10 February 2012).

[11] 'EU wants to be "catalyser" in climate change talk – Solana'. *AFP* [online], 25 June 2008. Available at http://afp.google.com/article/ALeqM5hq0DQuO-CAgjjuEQY3RwjK5Gow4g (accessed 10 February 2012).

References

Agh, A. (2010) Regionalisation as a driving force of EU widening: Recovering from the EU 'Carrot Crisis' in the 'East', *Europe–Asia Studies*, 62(8), pp. 1239–1266.

Ashton, C. (2011) The EU wants 'deep democracy' to take root in Egypt and Tunisia, *The Guardian*. Available at http://www.guardian.co.uk/commentisfree/2011/feb/04/egypt-tunisia-eu-deep-democracy (accessed 6 March 2012).

Averre, D. (2009) Competing rationalities: Russia, the EU – and the 'shared neighbourhood', *Europe–Asia Studies*, 61(10), pp. 1689–1703.

Bengtsson, R. & Elgström, O. (2012) Conflicting role conceptions? The European Union in global politics, *Foreign Policy Analysis*, 8(1), pp. 93–108.

Bickerton, C. J. (2011) *European Union Foreign Policy: From effectiveness to functionality* (Basingstoke: Palgrave Macmillan).

Biscop, S. (2010) The ENP, security and democracy in the context of the European security strategy, in: R. G. Whitman & S. Wolff (Eds) *The European Neighbourhood Policy in Perspective: Context, implementation and impact*, pp. 73–88 (London: Palgrave Macmillan).

Christou, G. (2010) European Union security logics to the east: The European Neighbourhood Policy and the Eastern Partnership, *European Security*, 19(3), pp. 413–430.

Cichocki, M. (2010) European neighbourhood policy or neighbourhood policies?, in: K. Henderson & C. Weaver (Eds) *The Black Sea Region and EU Policy: The challenge of divergent agendas*, pp. 9–28 (Surrey: Ashgate).

Cooper, R. (2007) *The Breaking of Nations: Order and chaos in the twenty-first century* (New York: Atlantic Books).

Council of the European Union (2003) *A Secure Europe in a Better World – European Security Strategy*. Brussels, 12 December.

Council of the European Union (2007) *Council Decision: Establishing a community civil protection mechanism (recast)*. 2007/779/EC, Euratom, Brussels, 8 November.

Council of the European Union (2008a) *Council Conclusions on European Neighbourhood Policy*. 2851st External Relations Council meeting, Brussels, 18 February.

Council of the European Union (2008b) *Report on the Implementation of the European Security Strategy – Providing Security in a Changing World*. S407/08, Brussels, 11 December.

Council of the European Union (2011) Joint Declaration of the Eastern Partnership Summit. 14983/11 PRESSE 341, Warsaw, 29–30 September.

Cox, R. W. (1981) Social forces, states and world orders: Beyond international relations theory, *Millennium – Journal of International Studies*, 10(2), pp. 126–155.

Delanty, G. & Rumford, C. (2005) *Rethinking Europe: Social theory and the implications of Europeanization* (London: Routledge).

Deutsch, K. W. (1966) *Nationalism and Social Communication: Inquiry into the foundations of nationality* (Cambridge: MIT Press).
Devatak, R. (1995) Incomplete states: Theories and practices of statecraft, in: J. MacMillan & A. Linklater (Eds) *Boundaries in Question: New directions on international relations*, pp. 30–48 (London: Pinter).
Diez, T. (2005) Constructing the self and changing others: Reconsidering 'normative power Europe', *Millennium – Journal of International Studies*, 33(3), pp. 613–636.
Eder, K. (2007) The public sphere and European democracy: Mechanism of democratization in the transnational situation, in: J. E. Fossum & P. Schlesinger (Eds) *The European Union and the Public Sphere: A communicative space in the making?*, pp. 47–65 (London: Routledge).
Entman, R. M. (1993) Framing: Toward clarification of a fractured paradigm, *Journal of Communication*, 43(4), pp. 51–58.
Eriksen, E. O. (2007) Conceptualizing European public spheres, in J. E. Fossum & P. Schlesinger (Eds) *The European Union and the Public Sphere: A communicative space in the making?*, pp. 121–139 (London: Routledge).
European Commission (2000) *White Paper on European Governance – 'Enhancing Democracy in the European Union'*, SEC(2000) 1547/7 final, Brussels, 11 October.
European Commission (2006) *White Paper on a European Communication Policy*. COM(2006) 35 final, Brussels, 1 February.
European Commission (2007) *Eurobarometre 66*. Brussels, September.
European Commission (2008) *Climate change and international security*. S113/08. Brussels, 14 May.
European Commission (2009) White Paper: Adapting to climate change: Towards a European framework for action. COM(2009) 147 final, Brussels, 14 April.
European Commission (2010a) *International climate policy post-Copenhagen; Acting now to reinvigorate global action on climate change*. S86/10, Brussels, June.
European Commission (2010b) *Special Eurobarometre 343 on Humanitarian aid*. Brussels, July.
European Commission High Representative (2011a) *Remarks on 'The EU Response to the Arab Spring'*. SPEECH/11/524, Washington: The Brookings Institution, 12 July.
European Commission High Representative (2011b) *Speech by European Union High Representative for Foreign Affairs and Security Policy Catherine Ashton on the Common Security and Defence Policy in the European Parliament*. SPEECH/11/524, Strasbourg: European Parliament, 13 December.
European Parliament (2010) Towards an EU peace-building strategy. Directorate – General for External Policies of the Union. EXPO/B/AFET/FWC/2009-01/Lot6/04, Brussels, April.
Falkner, R. (2007) The political economy of 'normative power' Europe: EU – environmental leadership in international biotechnology regulation, *Journal of European Public Policy*, 14(4), pp. 507–523.
Fossum, J. E. & Schlesinger, P. (Eds) (2007) *The European Union and the public sphere: A communicative space in the making?* (London: Routledge).
Fraser, N. (2007) Transnationalizing the public sphere: On the legitimacy and efficacy of public opinion in a post-Westphalian world, *Theory, Culture & Society*, 24(4), pp. 7–30.
Fuchs, D. (2011) Cultural diversity, European identity and legitimacy of the EU: A theoretical framework, in: D. Fuchs & H. D. Klingemann (Eds) *Cultural Diversity, European Identity and the Legitimacy of the EU*, pp. 27–59 (Cheltenham: Edward Elgar).
Goode, L. (2005) *Jurgen Habermas: Democracy and the public sphere* (London: Pluto Press).
Haas, E. B. (1958) *The uniting of Europe; Political, social, and economic forces, 1950–1957* (New York: Stanford University Press).
Harris, P. G. (2007) Sharing the burdens of global climate change: International equity and justice in European policy, in: P. G. Harris (Ed.) *Europe and Global Climate Change: Politics, foreign policy and regional cooperation*, pp. 99–118 (Cheltenham: Edward Elgar Publishing).
Haukkala, H. (2008) The European Union as a regional normative hegemon: The case of European neighbourhood policy, *Europe-Asia Studies*, 60(9), pp. 1601–1622.
Hill, C. (1993) The capability-expectations gap, or conceptualizing Europe's international role, *Journal of Common Market Studies*, 31(3), pp. 305–328.
Hoffmann, S. (1977) An American social science: International relations, *Daedalus*, 106(3), pp. 41–60.
Juncos, A. E. & Pomorska, K. (2011) Invisible and unaccountable? National Representatives and Council Officials in EU foreign policy, *Journal of European Public Policy*, 18(8), pp. 1096–1114.
Kantner, C. & Liberatore, A. (2006) Security and democracy in the European Union: An introductory framework, *European Security*, 15(4), pp. 363–383.

Kelemen, R. D. (2010) Globalizing European Union environmental policy, *Journal of European Public Policy*, 17 (3), pp. 335–349.

Kelemen, R. D. & Vogel, D. (2009) Trading places: The role of the United States and the European Union in international environmental politics, *Comparative Political Studies*, 43(4), pp. 427–456.

Krzyżanowski, M., Wodak, R. & Triandafyllidou, A. (2009) Introduction, in: A. R. Triandafyllidou, R. Wodak, & M. Krzyanowski (Eds) *The European Public Sphere and the Media: Europe in crisis*, pp. 1–21 (Basingstoke: Ashgate).

Laclau, E. & Mouffe, C. (2001) *Hegemony and Socialist Strategy: Towards a radical democratic politics* (London: Verso)

Linklater, A. (2007) Public spheres and civilizing processes. *Theory, Culture & Society*, 24(4), pp. 31–37.

Manners, I. (2010) Global Europa: Mythology of the European Union in world politics, *JCMS: Journal of Common Market Studies*, 48(1), pp. 67–87.

Nash, K. (2007) Transnationalizing the public sphere, *Theory, Culture & Society*, 24(4), pp. 53–57.

Paterson, M. (2009) Post-hegemonic climate politics?, *British Journal of Politics & International Relations*, 11(1), pp. 140–158.

President of the European Commission (2005) *Speech by EU Commission President Barroso: The EU and US: A declaration of interdependence*. SPEECH05/417. Washington: School of Advanced International Studies, 18 October.

President of the European Commission (2010) *Statement following the meeting with the President of Bulgaria Georgi Parvanov*. SPEECH10/41. Brussels, 23 February.

Schmidt, J. R. (2008) Why Europe leads on climate change, *Survival: Global Politics and Strategy*, 50(4), pp. 83–99.

Schmidt, V. A. (2008) Discursive institutionalism: The explanatory power of ideas and discourse, *Political Science*, 11(1), pp. 303–321.

Smith, M. E. (2011) A liberal grand strategy in a realist world? Power, purpose and the EU's changing global role, *Journal of European Public Policy*, 18(2), pp. 144–163.

Stråth, B. & Wodak, R. (2009) Europe – discourse – politics – media – history: Constructing 'crises'?, in: A. Triandafyllidou, R. Wodak, & M. Krzyżanowski (Eds) *The European Public Sphere and the Media: Europe in Crisis*, pp. 81–102 (Basingstoke: Palgrave Macmillan).

Tonra, B. (2010) Identity construction through the ENP: Borders and boundaries, insiders and outsiders, in: R. G. Whitman & S. Wolff (Eds) *The European Neighbourhood Policy in Perspective: Context, implementation and impact*, pp. 51–72 (London: Palgrave Macmillan).

Tonra, B. (2011) Democratic foundations of EU foreign policy: Narratives and the myth of EU exceptionalism, *Journal of European Public Policy*, 18(8), pp. 1190–1207.

Tonra, B. & Christiansen, T. (2005) *Rethinking European Union Foreign Policy* (Manchester: Manchester University Press).

Wagner, W. (2007) The democratic deficit in the Union's security and defense policy: Why bother? Paper presented at the 10th EUSA Biennial International Conference, Montreal.

Wolczuk, K. (2010) Convergence without finalité: EU strategy towards post-Soviet states in the wider Black Sea region, in: K. Henderson & C. Weaver (Eds) *The Black Sea Region and EU Policy: The challenge of divergent agendas*, pp. 45–63 (Surrey: Ashgate).

Wolf, K. D. (1999) The new raison d'état as a problem for democracy in world society, *European Journal of International Relations*, 5(3), pp. 333–363.

Youngs, R. (2010) *The European Union and Democracy Promotion: A critical global assessment* (Baltimore: The Johns Hopkins University Press).

Zielonka, J. (2007) *Europe as Empire: The nature of the Enlarged European Union* (Oxford: Oxford University Press).

The EU and Russia: Competing Discourses, Practices and Interests in the Shared Neighbourhood

VANDA AMARO DIAS
School of Economics, University of Coimbra, Portugal

ABSTRACT *This article analyses how the European Union (EU) and Russia perceive each other as regional players, by assessing their security-oriented policies towards the shared neighbourhood in Eastern Europe and South Caucasus, and delves into the impact those perceptions have on EU–Russia relations. It argues that both EU and Russian policies towards the region are built upon the belief that internal security starts outside their borders and, thus, the countries in the shared neighbourhood emerge as lynchpins in their internal and regional security strategies. In a mostly competing and mutually exclusive logic, the EU and Russia attempt to keep those countries in their own sphere of influence. Accordingly, commitments to European integration are generally seen by Moscow as a political loss, in the same way that a rapprochement towards Russia is usually perceived to constrain the EU's leverage in the region. This research is framed by a critical constructivist approach focusing on practices and discourses, thereby enabling a broader mapping of the dynamics resulting from the EU's and Russia's competing interests, perceptions and policies in the shared neighbourhood, and a deeper understanding of their impact on EU–Russia bilateral relations, particularly under the so-called strategic partnership.*

Introduction

Since the European Union's (EU) last rounds of enlargement, the Union and Russia share a common neighbourhood in Eastern Europe and South Caucasus. The fact that the EU is extending its power towards the post-Soviet space – an area traditionally perceived to be part of Moscow's sphere of influence – has significantly impacted on regional dynamics of power produced by and reflected on the interplay between interests, discourses and practices in this area. The resulting geopolitical transformation in the region has also affected perceptions about the geostrategic importance of the shared neighbourhood to the EU's and Russia's security, as well as their perceptions of each other as regional actors, not without consequences in EU–Russia bilateral relations.

Within this broader framework, this article envisages to analyse how the EU and Russia perceive each other as regional players by assessing their security-oriented policies towards the shared neighbourhood. In addition, the paper delves into the impact those perceptions and policies have on EU–Russia relations. The argument is made that both EU and Russian policies towards the region are built upon the belief that internal security starts outside their borders and, thus, the countries in the shared neighbourhood emerge as lynchpins in their internal and regional security strategies. In this sense, both the EU and Russia attempt to keep these countries in their own sphere of influence for security reasons, in a mostly competing and mutually exclusive logic. Although this perception of competition is transversal to EU–Russia relations overall – even if in different visibilities and intensities across sectors (Casier, 2012) – it becomes particularly evident in areas concerning the shared neighbourhood, because commitments to European integration of those countries are usually seen by Moscow as a political loss, in the same way that a rapprochement towards Russia is perceived to have a constraining effect over the EU's leverage in the region. In a time when the EU is struggling with a deep economic and financial crisis – that is affecting people's confidence in the process of European integration and its potential to assure peace and stability in Europe and its surroundings alike – and Russia is suffering the effects of an acute economic decline – prompting for a more cautious foreign policy and lower-cost sphere of influence (Judah et al., 2011, p. 9) – it is more crucial than ever to critically discuss their foreign, security and neighbouring policies and analyse how they affect EU–Russia relations and European peace and security overall.

In order to delve into the above-identified competing regional approaches and their impact on EU–Russia relations, the article proceeds as follows. Firstly, it presents the critical constructivist approach that frames the research. Critical constructivism provides a wide-range of tools to understand the link between interests, discourses and perceptions, as well as their influence on power and security. Moreover, it sheds light on the fact that reality is a dynamic construction in which actors adapt themselves to the demands of the moment, redefining interests and perceptions of their contextual environment whenever necessary. Unlike conventional approaches, this framework provides important avenues into the study of relational aspects of identity and the possibilities for change and transformation that enables us to map the dynamics resulting from the EU and Russia competing interests, perceptions and policies in the shared neighbourhood. Secondly, the article analyses the EU and Russia perceptions and policies towards their common vicinity, focusing on the security dimension. For that purpose it maps the evolution of EU and Russian policies towards the region and assesses how these two actors have conceptualized the shared neighbourhood as a lynchpin in their internal and regional security strategies. Finally, it explores the impact those perceptions and policies have on EU–Russia bilateral relations, particularly under the so-called strategic partnership, to identify how the interplay between discourses of power and regional security strategies have resulted in a mostly competing and mutually exclusive logic between these two actors over the shared neighbourhood.

Critical Constructivism: Framing the EU's and Russia's Security Approaches Towards the Shared Neighbourhood

Discourse critical constructivism is a strand of social constructivism – a social theory applied to IR since the late 1980s – inspired by postmodern authors such as Foucault, Derrida and Lyotard (Fierke & Jørgensen, 2001, p. 5). It shares with other strands of social constructivism the assumption that the human world is an artifice, i.e., a social construction. However, it is distinguished from them in that it embarked on a double – sociological and linguistic – turn and assumed itself as an interpretative post-positivist approach (Laffey & Weldes, 1997). Critical constructivism, one may argue, has also assumed a practical turn, in the sense that it understands the world as the result of 'praxis'. The focus on practices is helpful for it broadens the scope of analysis beyond text and meaning, interweaving together the material and discursive worlds – as practices are understood to be both material and meaningful – and, thus, engaging with structure–agent interactions and the processes of change and transformation (Adler & Pouliot, 2011). Assuming its post-positivist ontology, it makes possible to look at discourses and actions as social constructions, mirroring agents' power, understandings and interests (Kratochwil, 2001, pp. 16–20), and enabling a critical analysis of their practical consequences.

This results from the fact that critical constructivism assumes relations to be time-evolving and mutually constitutive (Fierke, 2007, p. 171). In this process, discourses turn out to be crucial for it is the ability to communicate that makes possible to socialize and imprint actions with meaning: diffusing perceptions of the 'self' and the 'other', establishing relations of power and redefining interests (Adler, 1997, p. 332). As a consequence, discourses and practices are perceived to be inextricably linked in the form of discursive practices. On the other hand, discourses are themselves structures reflecting a hegemonic understanding of social reality and they have a constitutive effect, disciplining and making interaction and decision-making possible (Simmerl, 2011, pp. 3–6). Therefore, while not underestimating the role of structures in defining agents' behaviour, critical constructivism allows the possibility of transformation to be included into the analysis of social reality by arguing that agents are capable of changing structures (Fierke, 2001, p. 123).

All in all, critical constructivism underlines the endogenous and exogenous factors that inform the process of decision-making and influence agent–structure interactions (Andreatta, 2005, p. 31). Nonetheless, although the impact of (discursive) structures on decision-making is recognized, structures are not reified but instead interpreted as social, historical and discursive (and changeable) constructions (Copeland, 2006, p. 7). From the agent–structure interaction results a process of social learning whose effects are felt not only in actors' identity formation but also on the perception of their interests (Checkel, 1999, p. 548). Therefore, critical constructivism highlights the fact that interests are themselves dynamic social constructions – opposed to given material conditions – that evolve according to actors' perceptions (Guzzini, 2000). To sum up, 'our ideas about ourselves and our environment shape our interactions and are shaped by our interactions; thereby they create social reality' (Zehfuss, 2001, p. 55).

In this framework, power and (in)security are also seen as dynamic social constructions where discourses, perceptions and interactions perform leading roles (Fierke, 2007, pp. 6–7). As a result, threats arise as the output of discursive practices and not as natural or pre-social elements (Zehfuss, 2006, p. 97). Changes in (auto)perceptions allow to track changes in actors' (in)securities, as well as different dynamics in relations with other actors (Bilgin,

2010). Moreover, critical constructivism conceives power as having a dimension of productiveness and possibility, based on ideas and norms, that becomes meaningful through discursive practices and, thus, is to be found everywhere (Burke, 2008, p. 363). As a result, power becomes the imposition of one vision of the world, determining shared meanings that contribute to build actors' interests, discourses and practices. The result is the ability to establish the rules of the game and persuade others to accept them, resulting in a hegemonic – and asymmetrical – social order (Adler, 1997, p. 336).

Methodologically, critical constructivism leans towards process tracing and critical discourse analysis. Process tracing is important to identify the broader social scenario within which relationships take place, 'who is interacting with whom or who is a source of concern for whom, and begin to piece together a map of identities and practices' (Fierke, 2001, p. 129). On its turn, critical discourse analysis enables a critical interpretation of the identified trends and patterns of behaviour. Here it is important to take into account that discourses are structures of signification, which construct social realities and binary oppositional relations of power where one member tends to be – or aims at being – privileged or hegemonic, thus creating asymmetrical relationships. In identifying and explaining these discourses we will be able to critically question and expose the practices they sustain, tackling dynamics that would otherwise remain invisible. The combination of these two methods will allow us to analyse how the EU and Russia bring meaning to their identities, practices and interactions, therefore recognizing the larger inter-subjective context within which both of them act and to draw conclusions based on the analysis of the relationship between the discursive practices of these actors and their outcome. Whilst the analysis of the position of the shared neighbourhood in this process would certainly contribute to a better and more comprehensive understanding of these dynamics, it would require more room for discussion than the scope of this article allows. Hence, while recognizing that the neighbourhood plays a meaningful role in these interactions, what will be under analysis here is the interplay between two sets of discursive practices that aim to become hegemonic, i.e., EU and Russian security-oriented policies towards the shared neighbourhood.

For that purpose, the next section tracks the development and evolution of these policies and the importance of the shared neighbourhood to the EU and Russian security strategies, while the final section analyses how these practices, and the perceptions and discourses they produce, influence EU–Russia bilateral relations.

EU and Russian Perceptions, Interests and Policies in the Shared Neighbourhood

European Union: Pursuing Power and Security in the Neighbourhood

The relations with neighbouring countries in Eastern Europe and South Caucasus have always been a significant part of the EU's post-Cold War foreign and security policies. During the 1990s it celebrated Association Agreements with candidate neighbours and Partnership and Cooperation Agreements with former Soviet States without membership prospects. However, the great bulk of attention was devoted to the Enlargement process. It was not until the creation of the European Neighbourhood Policy (ENP) in 2004 that the EU started to pay greater attention to the states in the shared neighbourhood with Russia (Casier, 2012, pp. 32–33). Since then, the EU's approach towards its eastern vicinity can be interpreted as an extension of the internal 'European project' aiming at preserving its security, stability and prosperity (Averre, 2009, pp. 1693–1694), because the EU perceives events in the region as having a direct impact on its internal order.

The ENP was developed to deal with the new security challenges at the EU's borders after the last rounds of enlargement (Jeandesboz, 2007, p. 397). In fact, there was nothing new about the challenges in the region, but the transformation of the EU's contextual environment triggered a process of change in its perceived threats. Consequently, the EU's interests in the neighbourhood were redefined and new political discourses were constructed to establish new relations of power and persuade the countries in the shared neighbourhood to adopt EU norms and values, thus contributing to reinforce its security.

Operationalized through Actions Plans and complemented by a wide range of trade and assistance programmes, the ENP intends to create a 'ring of friends' around the EU, 'avoid new dividing lines in Europe', and 'promote stability and prosperity' across the continent (Communication from the Commission, 2003). Its foundational basis can be traced back to the European Security Strategy (ESS), a document – adopted in 2003 and reinforced in 2008 (European Council, 2008) – acknowledging that enlargement brought the EU closer to troubled areas and the need to promote stability and good governance in the immediate EU neighbourhood (European Council, 2003). It highlights that 'the internal and external aspects of security are indissolubly linked' (European Council, 2003, p. 2) and, therefore, the EU's security interests cannot be untied from its overall approach to the neighbourhood (Browning & Joenniemi, 2008, p. 520). In this sense, the European peace and security argument becomes one of the most important rationales of the EU's neighbouring policies (Higashino, 2004, p. 347). This is particularly clear in the ESS when it states:

> The best protection for our security is a world of well-governed democratic states. Spreading good governance, supporting social and political reform, dealing with corruption and abuse of power, establishing the rule of law and protecting human rights are the best means of strengthening the international order. (European Council, 2003, p. 10)

Since the launch of the Eastern Partnership (EaP) initiative in 2009 – a few months after the war between Georgia and Russia – the EU has been trying to assume a greater regional role, increasing its strategic importance for the neighbourhood (Council of the European Union, 2009, p. 6). The goal is to extend the EU's power eastwards, therefore – though not explicitly – challenging and constraining Russian leverage over the region. Officially, the initiative's main goal is to promote socio-economic reforms and further political dialogue in and with the six participating countries: Armenia, Azerbaijan, Belarus, Georgia, Moldova and Ukraine. In practice, however, the EU is promoting the harmonization of their legal systems with the EU's *acquis communautaire* and creating favourable conditions for political integration through 'shared values' (Tumanov et al., 2011, p. 130), with the ultimate goal of ensuring the EU's security, as further stated in the ESS implementation report:

> The Eastern Partnership foresees a real step change in relations with our Eastern neighbours, with a significant upgrading of political, economic and trade relations. The goal is to strengthen the prosperity and stability of these countries, and thus the security of the EU. (European Council, 2008)

Additionally, the Joint Declaration of the Prague Eastern Partnership Summit affirms:

> The main goal of the Eastern Partnership is to create the necessary conditions to accelerate political association and further economic integration between the European Union and interested partner countries... This serves the shared commitment to stability, security and prosperity of the European Union, the partner countries and indeed the entire European continent. (Council of the European Union, 2009, p. 6)

These quotations suggest that: on the one hand, the EU projects its own security as being dependent on events in the region; on the other hand, for the EU, security in the neighbourhood is equated as the sum of economic prosperity and socio-political stability. To achieve these goals the EaP provides a dual-track approach combining the traditional bilateral relations between the EU and its neighbouring countries – that foresees their political association and economic integration with the EU – with a multilateral track that supports regional cooperation and the development of closer ties among the EaP partners (Council of the European Union, 2009, p. 6). The EU is currently negotiating Association Agreements that will replace the PCA, offering an extension of the economic and political benefits on the table, even if membership remains excluded from this framework.

The EU's overall approach towards its eastern vicinity relies heavily on positive conditionality and socialization, because the EU wants to promote its norms and values beyond its borders (Headley, 2012, p. 428). Accordingly, the EU offers a stance in its internal market and financial support to stimulate economic, political and social reforms, as well as security cooperation in the neighbourhood (Communication from the Commission, 2003, pp. 10–15), in order to address the root causes of instability, crisis and conflict. As a result, the EU's political and financial support to its neighbouring countries is used to persuade them to take the reforms that best suit the EU's security interests (Armstrong, 2007, p. 5). Alongside, the social learning processes resulting from institutional and people-to-people contacts and aiming at creating collective shared understanding of proper behaviour reveal, in practice, the EU's superiority within these (asymmetrical) relationships and its attempt to establish the rules of the game and impose its vision of the world over the neighbourhood. The consequence is a structural foreign policy seeking to influence and transform the political, economic and social systems of the EU's neighbours (Emerson, 2011, pp. 56–57): a *sine qua non* condition for the EU's extension of power over the shared neighbourhood, in order to preserve its own peace and security.

Russia: Struggling to Preserve Power and Security in the Near Abroad

In the early 1990s, Russia engaged in an internal debate on what were to be its national interests after the end of the Cold War. After a short romantic period when the need to develop close relations with the West featured prominently, it redefined its interests and decided that the near abroad was to be the main focus of Russian foreign policy (Trenin, 2009, p. 8). Similarly to the EU, Moscow's strategy towards the shared neighbourhood represents an extension of its internal project aiming to shape its external environment by establishing friendly states on its periphery as a *sine qua non* condition for domestic and regional security (Averre, 2009, pp. 1696–1697). Therefore, the internal and external dimensions of security are also indissolubly interlinked in Russian security and regional policies. According to the Foreign Policy Concept of the Russian Federation (2008): 'differences between domestic and external means of ensuring national interests and security are gradually disappearing' and thus the 'development of bilateral and multilateral cooperation with the CIS member states constitutes a priority area of Russia's foreign policy'.

Moscow looks at its vicinity as a sphere of privileged interests and a direct link to its internal development (Radchuk, 2011, p. 29) and international projection because it believes that it can only be a pole in a multipolar world if it has a sphere of influence (Judah et al., 2011, p. 23). Hence, Russia believes it has the right to intervene and control events in the post-Soviet space. For the same reason, it remains concerned towards the EU's increasing involvement in the region, for it fears that Brussels can persuade the countries in the shared neighbourhood to gravitate around the EU and NATO orbits, weakening Moscow's leverage in the region (Massari, 2007, p. 11). Therefore, for Moscow, security in the near abroad is the ability to have friendly regimes at its borders, regardless of their political orientations, that support Russian leadership at the regional level and its projection at the international level.

In the 2000s, after the election of Vladimir Putin for the presidency of the Russian Federation – facing a substantial economic recovery and the new assertiveness and pragmatism of its domestic and foreign policies – Russia has not hesitated to use its hard power in the shared neighbourhood with the EU (Isakova, 2005, pp. 17–18). The strategy has been to use Russian (economic, energetic, political and military) resources to increase the vulnerabilities and political, security and economic dependences of the countries in the region, allowing Russia to preserve asymmetric relations favouring the maintenance of these countries in its sphere of influence (Baev, 2007, p. 454). This rationale mirrors the geopolitical and geostrategic importance of the region to its security.

In the political realm, this strategy includes regional initiatives intended at preserving Russia's leadership in the post-Soviet space and assuring a political environment favourable to Russian interests, such as the Community of Independent States and the Collective Security Treaty Organisation, as well as support to pro-Russian political parties and non-governmental organizations in the near abroad (Tolstrup, 2009, pp. 932–933). In the military field, the presence of its troops across the region and Russia's prominent role in the protracted conflicts of the post-Soviet space have put a long strain on decision makers in the shared neighbourhood (Trenin, 2009, p. 11). Economically, Russia has developed several bilateral and multilateral attempts to integrate the markets in its periphery, such as the Single Economic Space. Simultaneously, it has steadily taken a share on the main economic sectors in the region (Tsygankov, 2006, pp. 147–148) increasing the levels of transactions and interdependence between Moscow and its vicinity, while requiring the maintenance of a political and economic secure environment for the success of Russian business and corporate activism. Moscow has also made use of differentiated energy prices, gas and food embargoes to project its hard power and explore the vulnerabilities of its neighbours, in order to reinforce its regional influence and increase the economic and political revenues to the Kremlin (Denisov & Grivach, 2008, p. 96).

Although in general Moscow deploys a more assertive strategy over the shared neighbourhood than the EU, Russian authorities have been increasingly resorting to soft power to enhance its economic attractiveness to promote stability and security in the region. Since 2004, after the coloured revolutions in Georgia and Ukraine, Russia has been paying more attention to its normative agenda. It perceived those events as western-sponsored movements for forced change in its privileged area of interests (Sakwa, 2011, p. 962) aiming at undermining its influence in the region. As a consequence, it has been promoting pro-Russian youth groups and non-governmental organizations in Russia and abroad, while presenting its own concept of democracy and freedom – 'sovereign democracy' – as an alternative to the liberal model enforced by the EU (Popescu & Wilson, 2009). Furthermore, discourses relating to the common civilizational and cultural legacy of the Soviet Union are often used to justify Russia's greatness and right to interfere in the near abroad (Makarychev, 2009, p. 55), thus working as structures of signification aiming at reinforcing its power in the region. Simultaneously, these discourses reveal that Moscow perceives the amity of its neighbours and the harmony of their political choices with Russian interests as a pivotal requirement to preserve its influence in the region and, consequently, guarantee Russia's domestic, regional and global security. Therefore, it combines an active hard power strategy with the advantages of the Soviet legacy to persuade the countries in the near abroad to comply with Russia's rules and vision of the world in order to preserve its regional leverage and internal security.

Competing for the Neighbourhood

This mapping exercise discloses that both the EU and Russia try to create links of interdependence with the countries in their vicinity – whether through conditionality and socialization, in the case of the EU, or the deepening of vulnerabilities in the region, in the case of Russia – because interdependence produces reciprocal, though asymmetrical, relations that can, potentially, create sources of influence (Casier, 2011, p. 497). Both of them want to extend their power over the region, imposing their vision of the world through a number of policies, initiatives and strategies, in order to establish the rules of the game and persuade the countries in the shared neighbourhood to accept asymmetrical relationships in which they are supposed to contribute to the security projects of these two regional actors. These competing approaches are also a cause of tension for the countries in the shared neighbourhood that find themselves torn between the attractions of the EU's agenda – which promises them technical aid, financial assistance and, eventually, a stake in the EU's single market – and a cooperative relationship with Russia – which many of these countries are overwhelmingly dependent on (Gower & Timmins, 2009, pp. 1685–1686). In this complex scenario, the EU is seen as a club that can create prosperity and stability, and for that reason it possesses considerable power of attraction to its neighbours (Feroci, 2011, p. 25) that tend to accept the EU's conditions and social behaviour in exchange for integration in the European project. Nonetheless, the complex and time-consuming nature of EU neighbouring policies open the way for Moscow to be viewed by the countries in Eastern Europe and South Caucasus as a power that can offer them immediate solutions to their problems, and for that reason they seem willing to overcome their differences (Nitoiu, 2011, pp. 463–467). Finding themselves in the middle of such competing dynamics, the countries in the shared neighbourhood tend to balance between the EU and Russia to satisfy their national interests, even if the capacity to do so varies considerably among these countries. Although they are not interested in upsetting any of the two regional giants (Tumanov et al., 2011, p. 129), this balancing has the potential to drag Russia and the EU into (indirect) confrontation, transforming the EU–Russia-shared neighbourhood triangle into a cornerstone cause of tension and a key feature of EU–Russia bilateral relations, as the following section reveals.

EU–Russia Relations: Strategic Partners or Regional Security Competitors?

The EU and Russia are two different partners with distinct, and sometimes incompatible, agendas: the EU is a regional organization with a multilevel system of decision-making where national and collective interests are not always easy to reconcile; and Russia is a traditional power with well-defined and focused foreign and regional interests, which are perceived to be vital for the country's internal cohesion and international projection (Freire, 2011, p. 139). As a result, EU–Russia relations have not always been easy as they are affected by the differences in the nature, and *modus operandi*, of Brussels and Moscow.

EU–Russia relations are partly framed by the PCA ratified in 1997, which established the structures for the development of: relations of partnership; political dialogue and economic, social and cultural co-operation. Furthermore, economic relations are shaped by the Agreement on Partnership and Cooperation establishing a partnership between the European Community and their member states, of one part, and the Russian Federation, of the other part (1997). In June 1999, the EU approved the Common Strategy on Russia (expired in 2004) stressing the strategic importance of the country to European security and the need to maintain a positive and constructive dialogue between the EU and Russia. As a response, in October 1999 Moscow presented the Medium-term Strategy for Development of Relations between the Russian Federation and the European Union that, in a very pragmatic tone, projects the image of Russia as a reliable partner, its commitment to the European security and the role the EU can perform in the country's modernization, democratization and economic development (Freire, 2011, pp. 141–142).

Russia's political assertiveness and economic growth in the 2000s affected the dynamics of its relations with the EU. From 2003 onwards the EU–Russia relationship gained a more pragmatic and practical dimension, meaning that any element of conditionality, imposed 'Europeanization' or attempt to interfere in Russian internal affairs would have Moscow's veto (Headley, 2012, p. 428). Furthermore, the Kremlin's self-exclusion from the ENP framework and the very concept of 'shared neighbourhood', which Russian leaders perceived as a threat from the West to what used to be Russia's traditional sphere of influence and direct challenging of Russian regional power, contributed to the creation of a competitive agenda between the EU and Russia over the region (Gower & Timmins, 2009, p. 1687). Reflecting this pragmatic security-focused turn, the 2003 St Petersburg EU–Russia summit established the goal to build four common spaces under the PCA framework: (1) economy; (2) freedom, security and justice; (3) external security; and (4) research and education (EU–Russia Summit, 2003). Additionally, in 2005 Russia and the EU adopted 'Road Maps' for implementing these common spaces and creating the 'infrastructure of a genuine strategic partnership' (Marsh, 2008, p. 185). However, this so-called strategic partnership remains too vague in its description of EU–Russia relations for the actual strategy behind it (strategic for whom? according to what parameters and whose perceptions?) and the exact understanding of partnership (is this an asymmetric or equal partnership?) remains unclear.

Behind this pragmatic turn was the perception that the EU enlargement eastwards implied a range of issues concerning the future shared neighbourhood that had to be dealt with through a working relationship (Flenley, 2008, pp. 198–199). The eastern enlargement added a level of complexity in EU–Russia relations that despite significant progress in several areas of technical cooperation have suffered from political ups and downs and mutual distrust. Given the historical past and memory of many of the EU's new member states, it became more difficult to reach common strategic decisions regarding Russia (Massari, 2007, p. 1). These countries tended to be critical and defensive vis-à-vis Russia and its approach towards the shared neighbourhood. That position is not shared by France and Germany, which have often pushed for a 'Russia-first' policy when dealing with the shared neighbourhood, blocking initiatives to strengthen the Eastern dimension of the ENP or include a membership perspective within the EaP (Nitoiu, 2011, pp. 463–465). These diverging approaches within the EU have hampered the effective promotion of its norms and values in both Russia and the shared neighbourhood, affecting perceptions concerning the coherence and effectiveness of EU foreign and neighbouring policies. However, this gap is shrinking as member states have been becoming less divided in their views and approaches towards Russia, particularly in the last couple of years, and are now calling for a joint EU approach to Russia based on shared interests and objectives (Judah et al., 2011, p. 50).

Nonetheless, one main problem is that both the EU and Russia want different things from their relationship. That is not only clear in the case of the strategic partnership but also in the case of more recent initiatives such as the Partnership for Modernisation launched in 2010. The purpose of this initiative is to modernize Russia's economy and political institutions, and foster interdependence between the EU and Russia (Council of the European Union, 2010). However, in practice, the EU and Russia have different goals in mind. Whereas for Moscow modernization is, above all, a matter of importing Western technology, know-how and investments, the EU conceives this partnership as a way of influencing and transforming Russian institutions (Judah et al., 2011, p. 53).

In general, EU–Russia relations have balanced between conflict and cooperation. The four common spaces established between the EU and Russia in 2003 lack practical content and remain largely a rhetorical commitment, though there are noteworthy exceptions. In the Common Economic Space and its ultimate goal of creating an open and integrated market between the EU and Russia (Road Map on the Common Economic Space, 2005), dialogue has been launched in a number of areas, especially in trade and energy that remain the central points in EU–Russia relations (Communication from the Commission, 2008, pp. 2–3). Cooperation in freedom, security and justice affairs seems the most promising though. The EU and Russia have signed agreements on visa facilitation, the fight against organized crime and terrorism. Furthermore, the EU is supporting border management and judiciary reform in Russia and Moscow has established technical cooperation with EU bodies, such as Frontex, Europol and Eurojust (Potemkina, 2010). Cooperation under the fourth common space has so far been translated into a few concrete steps, such as the creation of a co-funded Moscow Institute of European Studies and a number of exchange programmes – e.g., Erasmus Mundus – which widen the professional and personal contacts between societies (EU–Russia Common Spaces Progress Report, 2008, p. 45).

However, cooperation is particularly difficult and limited under the Common Space of External Security. Despite Russia's contribution to the EU's operation in Chad and Somalia (EU–Russia Common Spaces Progress Report, 2008, p. 3) and the creation of the EU–Russia Political and Security Committee in 2010 (Dettke, 2011, p. 128), in the external security field, the EU–Russia strategic partnership reveals a level of competition resulting from their divergent positions regarding the shared neighbourhood (Nitoiu, 2011, p. 462). Since 2004, EU regional policies in this area have been growing in number and scope strengthening the perception of the EU as a political and strategic actor in the region, whereas Russia understands the shared neighbourhood as its privileged sphere of influence and believes that, for that reason, EU foreign and security policies should not interfere in its vital area of interests (Massari, 2007, p. 9).

The mapping exercise done in the previous section revealed that both the EU and Russia are pursuing the same goal in the shared neighbourhood: extend their power and influence over the region in order to safeguard their internal security, stability and prosperity. Therefore, we are standing before two competing and mutually exclusive regional rationales and strategies that affect the bilateral EU–Russia relations. If initially the EU enlargement and neighbourhood policies were perceived by Moscow as a development approach to the region, today they are increasingly seen as a source of new challenges and rivalry in the post-Soviet space. Russia sees the EU's initiatives in the region as constraining its leverage in its traditional area of geopolitical and economic interests (Freire, 2011, p. 159). On its hand, the EU tends to perceive Moscow as a hostile power relying on the Cold War notion of spheres of influence, particularly whenever it tries to block the EU's neighbouring policies and initiatives (Trenin, 2009, pp. 3–4).

Consequently, the European and Russian elites have been competing to promote the legitimacy of their norms, political principles and regional approaches. The lenses of critical constructivism combined with process tracing and the critical analysis of discourses by these two actors provide, therefore, a comprehensive understanding of this scenario as a dynamic social interaction in which both the EU and Russia strive to impose their rules, visions of the world and security interests. The goal is to become the privileged party in an asymmetrical relationship, resulting in a hegemonic struggle for power and control over the shared neighbourhood.

The events in Georgia in 2008 have further worsened EU–Russia relations leading the EU to condemn Moscow for the violation of Georgia's territorial integrity with the use of force and the unilateral recognition of Abkhazia and south Ossetia. In the words of the Commissioner for External Relations and European Neighbourhood Policy, Benita Ferrero-Waldner, these events:

> … remain unacceptable, and we [the EU] cannot share the principles of foreign policy recently articulated in Moscow, including the resurgence of spheres of influence. So, the ongoing review [of EU–Russia relations] has to make a rather sober assessment of the EU's own self-interest in this relationship. (Ferrero-Waldner, 2008a)

Regarding the EaP initiative launched in 2009 as a response to the events in the region – not only the Russian–Georgian war but also the 2009 energy crisis with Ukraine – the Russian foreign minister Sergei Lavrov revealed his suspicion when he accused the EU of trying to carve out a new sphere of influence in Russia's own backyard and creating new dividing lines in Europe (Ria Novosti, 2009). The EU–Russia summit of 2009 exposed even further the mistrust and disagreement between the two sides, when President Medvedev suggested that 'the EU itself did not know yet why it needs the Eastern Partnership', even if stressing that he did not want the initiative 'to turn into a partnership against Russia' (Radio Free Europe/Radio Liberty, 2009). Furthermore, the EaP has had an important effect on Russian identity at least in two different, though inter-related, dimensions: first, it hurt Russia's aspirations to be recognized as the EU's primary partner in the region, because it identifies the countries in Eastern Europe and South Caucasus as the EU's closest partners; second, the EaP initiative reinforced the EU presence in Russia's traditional sphere of influence, thus challenging its regional power ambitions and affecting the narratives upon which Russia has been building its identity traits (Casier, 2012). Through the ENP and regional initiatives, such as the EaP, the EU has been not only overtaking Russia as the main partner of most countries in the shared neighbourhood, but it has also been increasing its role as a security actor in the region. In fact, the EU has started to play a more prominent role in the protracted conflicts in Transnistria and Georgia, therefore reducing Russia's room for manoeuvre and constraining its options in the region (Judah et al., 2011, p. 25).

For that reason, Russia remains suspicious of these policies and initiatives and accuses the EU's normative agenda of being as much about power, interests and influence as about values, which impose a choice on the countries of the shared neighbourhood (Averre, 2009, p. 1699). This image was reinforced by the coloured revolutions in the region, spreading a cynical view of the EU as imposing a certain model of governance that suits its interests – promotion of its own security and extension of its economic leverage over the eastern vicinity – which clashes directly with Moscow's own normative discourse about the shared neighbourhood, increasing the competition over this area (Flenley, 2008, p. 200). Therefore, both Brussels and Moscow attempt to block each other policies and strategies in the region because they perceive their approaches towards this space as mutually exclusive.

The competing discursive practices analysed here emerge as structures of action and signification whereby the EU and Russia try to reaffirm its – moral and political – superiority and prove the other as an unreliable partner. In this way they project the other as a threat and use that constructed image to attract the countries in the shared neighbourhood into their sphere of influence and persuade them to accept their exercise of power, as well as the terms of an asymmetrical relationship, in exchange for protection from this threatening 'other'.

Nevertheless, contentions over the shared neighbourhood do not mean that the EU and Russia have their backs turned on each other permanently. In fact, the official political rhetoric is far more cooperative than confrontational. Despite their regional competition, none of the parties believe that they are better off without each other; rather they recognize the need to deepen EU–Russia cooperation (Freire, 2011, p. 143). There are a number of practical evidences that support this rhetorical orientation, such as Russia's acceptance to comply with EU standards of governance in specific policy areas relevant to the internal market and the modernization of its political system.

The preservation of a cooperative voice in EU–Russia bilateral relations – even if it remains largely declaratory – mirrors the fact that European peace and security is complex and implies the interconnectedness of both Moscow and Brussels. Accordingly, the cost of negative attitudes towards Russia or the EU are significant and could further increase in the future (Baranovsky, 2010, p. 44) as security threats become more transnational, highlighting the blurring of internal and external dimensions of security. That is precisely the reason for the reluctance of the EU to become more politically involved in the shared neighbourhood and to clearly assume its security interests over the region, for it does not want to jeopardise its relations with Moscow. This rationale is evident in the speech of the former European Commissioner for External Relations and European Neighbourhood Policy, Benita Ferrero-Waldner:

> A strong Russia is positive for the European Union. If we are to tackle problems such as uncontrolled migration, climate change, drugs trafficking and cross-border crime, we need to do so with a prosperous and stable Russia... Greater instability in the region is clearly not in our mutual interest... We want to do this together with Russia. (Ferrero-Waldner, 2008b)

On the other hand, Russia is willing to cooperate with the EU on matters regarding their common interest in regional stability. However, it will only work in its own terms and not on supposedly shared interests and values previously defined by Brussels (Headley, 2012, p. 445). Even though Russia had to rethink its foreign policy approaches due to the economic crisis, Moscow also sees the EU as declining and thus will only accept to build a partnership on equal footing. This may be facilitated by a recent trend inside the EU – largely propelled by a crisis of confidence shaped by the economic and financial turmoil – to abandon its transformative ambition regarding Russia, and to assume a more pragmatic approach towards its relations with Moscow, meaning that the EU seems willing to assume Russia as a partner with which the EU wants to do business, but does not try to change (Judah et al., 2011, p. 49). These cooperative discursive practices shed light on the dynamic character of EU–Russia relations and the fact that Moscow and Brussels have the ability to adapt themselves to the needs and demands of the moment and refine their words and deeds accordingly.

However, the power games and dynamics between the EU and Russia have often been more visible in forms different from this cooperative one, whenever their 'privileged' interests – the need to secure their peripheries as a condition for internal security and stability – are on the table, revealing that EU–Russia relations result from the sensitive and difficult balance between a strategic partnership with a cooperative tone and a regional competition for influence, power and security.

Concluding Remarks

Critical constructivism and its focus on the linkages between perceptions, discourses and practices, as well as their influences on power and security provide important avenues into the study of EU–Russia relations. Following this framework of analysis this article revealed the shared neighbourhood as a cornerstone cause of tension between these two regional powers and how this tension is reflected in their bilateral relations.

By focusing on the analysis of practices and discourses this article allowed for a broader mapping of the dynamics resulting from EU and Russian neighbouring policies and revealed that, to some extent, both the EU and Russia want to reach the same goal in the shared neighbourhood: expand their influence and reinforce the exercise of power in the region in order to safeguard their internal security, stability and prosperity, while increasing their global power and international projection. In this complex scenario, the EU's agenda revolved around extending its power eastwards and deepening the economic and political integration of the countries in the shared neighbourhood, whereas Russia has been seeking to explore vulnerabilities in the region in order to restore its national, regional and global power and to reassert its influence in the post-Soviet space. The result is a competition between two regional rationales – and hegemonic ambitions over the shared neighbourhood – that has an important impact on EU–Russia bilateral relations.

These diverging positions result in the distrust and misunderstanding that imprint the EU–Russia agenda and lead these actors to block each other's initiatives, because they perceive their competition over the shared neighbourhood as being mutually exclusive. However, these dynamics become further complicated by the EU's and Russia's awareness of the need to cooperate in a number of fields. The political discourse emphasizes the cooperative orientation of EU–Russia relations revealing the European security's complex nature and the need for a joint EU–Russia strategy to address common threats. Therefore, the relations between the EU and Russia are not always mutually exclusive as both actors are willing to cooperate to address common challenges, such as regional stabilization, economic development or security enhancement in their shared neighbourhood. Ultimately, the cost of negative attitudes towards Russia or the EU is significant and somewhat restrains these actors to compete aggressively and directly over the shared neighbourhood. As a result, EU–Russia relations revolve around a complex, and sometimes schizophrenic, balance between strategic partnership and regional competition, which reveals the dynamic and changeable nature of this relationship, as well as Moscow's and Brussels' ability to adapt their discourses and practices – and perceptions of the 'other' – according to their contextual environment and perceived interests at a given moment.

Acknowledgments

I would like to thank Maria Raquel Freire, Cristian Nitoiu and Nikola Tomic for their insightful comments on early drafts of this paper.

I am also grateful for the funding provided under the Marie Curie SPBUILD Initial Training Network Fellowship of the European Community's Seventh Framework Program.

References

Adler, E. (1997) Seizing the middle ground: Constructivism in world politics, *European Journal of International Relations*, 3(3), pp. 319–363.

Adler, E. & Pouliot, V. (2011) International practices, *International Theory*, 3(1), pp. 1–36.

Agreement on Partnership and Cooperation establishing a partnership between the European Community and their member states, of one part, and the Russian Federation, of the other part (1997) OJ L327, 28/11/1997, pp. 3–70.

Andreatta, F. (2005) Theory and the European Union's international relations, in: C. Hill & M. Smith (Eds) *International Relations and the European Union*, pp. 18–38 (Oxford: Oxford University Press).

Armstrong, W. (2007) Introduction: Borders in an unequal world, in: W. Armstrong, Warwick & J. Anderson (Eds) *Geopolitics of European Union Enlargement: The fortress empire*, pp. 1–8 (London: Routledge).

Averre, D. (2009) Competing rationalities: Russia, the EU and the shared neighbourhood, *Europe–Asia Studies*, 61(10), pp. 1689–713.

Baev, P. K. (2007) Russia aspires to the status of 'energy superpower', *Strategic Analysis*, 31(3), pp. 447–465.

Baranovsky, V. (2010) Russia's approach to security building in the Euro-Atlantic Zone, *The International Spectator: Italian Journal of International Affairs*, 45(2), pp. 41–53.

Bilgin, P. (2010) Identity/security, in: J. P. Burgess (Ed.) *The Routledge Handbook of New Security Studies*, pp. 81–89 (London: Routledge).

Browning, C. S. & Joenniemi, P. (2008) Geostrategies of the European Neighbourhood Policy, *European Journal of International Relations*, 14(3), pp. 519–551.

Burke, A. (2008) Postmodernism, in: C. Reus-Smit & D. Snidal (Eds) *The Oxford Handbook of International Relations*, pp. 359–377 (Oxford: Oxford University Press).

Casier, T. (2011) Russia's energy leverage over the EU: Myth or reality?, *Perspectives on European Politics and Society*, 12(4), pp. 494–508.
Casier, T. (2012) Are the policies of Russia and the EU in their shared neighbourhood doomed to clash?, in: R. Kanet & M. R. Freire (Eds) *Competing for Influence: The EU and Russia in post-Soviet Eurasia*, pp. 31–53 (The Netherlands: Republic of Letters).
Checkel, J. T. (1999) Social construction and integration, *Journal of European Public Policy*, 6(4), pp. 545–560.
Communication from the Commission to the Council (2008) *Review of EU–Russia Relations*. COM (2008) 740 final.
Communication from the Commission to the Council and the European Parliament (2003) *Wider Europe – Neighbourhood: A new framework for relations with our eastern and southern neighbours*. COM (2003) 104 final.
Copeland, D. C. (2006) The constructivism challenge to structural realism: A review essay, in: S. Guzzini & A. Leander (Eds) *Constructivism and International Relations: Alexander Wendt and his critics*, pp. 1–20 (London: Routledge).
Council of the European Union (2009) *Joint Declaration of the Prague Eastern Partnership Summit*. Prague, 7 May, 8435/09 (Presse 78).
Council of the European Union (2010) *Joint Statement on the Partnership for Modernisation EU–Russia Summit*. Rostov-on-Don, 1 June. 10546/10 (Presse 154).
Denisov, A. & Grivach, A. (2008) The gains and failures of the energy superpower, *Russia in Global Affairs*, 6(2), pp. 96–108.
Dettke, D. (2011) Europe and Russia: From neighborhood without a shared vision to a modernization partnership, *European Security*, 20(1), pp. 127–142.
Emerson, M. (2011) Just good friends? The European Union's multiple neighbourhood policies, *The International Spectator*, 46(4), pp. 45–62.
European Council (2003) *European Security Strategy: A secure Europe in a better world*. Brussels, 12 December.
European Council (2008) *Report on the Implementation of the European Security Strategy – Providing Security in a Changing World*. S407/08, Brussels, 11 December.
EU Russia Common Spaces Progress Report (2008) Available at http://eeas.europa.eu/russia/docs/commonspaces_prog_report_2008_en.pdf (accessed 1 June 2012).
EU–Russia Summit (2003) Joint statement. St Petersburg, 31 May. Available at http://www.consilium.europa.eu/uedocs/cms_data/docs/pressdata/en/er/75969.pdf (accessed 1 June 2012).
Feroci, F. N. (2011) EU enlargement policy: From success to fatigue, in: F. Bindi & I. Angelescu (Eds) *The Frontiers of Europe: A transatlantic problem?*, pp. 25–34 (Washington, DC: The Brookings Institution and Scuola Superiore della Pubblica Amministrazione (SPPA)).
Ferrero-Walner, B. (2008a) *EP plenary debate on EU/Russia – EU/Russia: A challenging partnership, but one of the most important of our times*. 21 October. Available at http://europa.eu/rapid/pressReleasesAction.do?reference=SPEECH/08/545&format=HTML&aged=0&language=EN&guiLanguage=en (accessed 1 June 2012).
Ferrero-Waldner, B. (2008b) *Speech at the European Club, State Duma: Russia and the EU need each other*. 4 June. Available at http://europa.eu/rapid/pressReleasesAction.do?reference=SPEECH/08/300&type=HTML (accessed 1 June 2012).
Fierke, K. M. (2001) Critical methodology and constructivism, in: K. M. Fierke & K. E. Jørgensen (Eds) *Constructing International Relations: The next generation*, pp. 115–135 (New York: M. E. Sharpe).
Fierke, K. M. (2007) *Critical Approaches to International Security* (Cambridge: Polity Press).
Fierke, K. M. & Jørgensen, K. E. (2001) Introduction, in: K. M. Fierke & K. E. Jørgensen (Eds) *Constructing International Relations: The next generation*, pp. 3–10 (New York: M. E. Sharpe).
Flenley, P. (2008) Russia and the EU: The clash of new neighbourhoods?, *Journal of Contemporary European Studies*, 16(2), pp. 189–202.
Freire, M. R. (2011) *A Rússia de Putin: Vectores Estruturantes de Política Externa* (Coimbra: Almedina).
Gower, J. & Timmins, G. (2009) Introduction: The European Union, Russia and the shared neighbourhood, *Europe–Asia Studies*, 61(10), pp. 1685–1687.
Guzzini, S. (2000) Reconstruction of constructivism in international relations, *European Journal of International Relations*, 6(2), pp. 147–182.
Headley, J. (2012) Is russia out of step with European norms? Assessing Russia's relationship to European identity, values and norms through the issue of self-determination, *Europe–Asia Studies*, 64(3), pp. 427–447.

Higashino, A. (2004) Sake of 'peace and security'? The role of security in the European Union enlargement eastwards, *Cooperation and Conflict*, 39(4), pp. 347–368.

Isakova, I. (2005) *Russian Governance in the Twenty-first Century* (London: Frank Cass).

Jeandesboz, J. (2007) Labelling the 'neighbourhood': Towards a genesis of the European neighbourhood policy, *Journal of International Relations and Development*, 10(4), pp. 387–416.

Judah, B., Kobzova, J. & Popescu, N. (2011) *Dealing with a Post-BRIC Russia* (London: European Council on Foreign Relations).

Kratochwil, F. V. (2001) Constructivism as an approach to interdisciplinary Study, in: K. M. Fierke & K. E. Jørgensen (Eds) *Constructing International Relations: The next generation*, pp. 13–35 (New York: M. E. Sharpe).

Laffey, M. & Weldes, J. (1997) Beyond belief: Ideas and symbolic technologies in the study of international relations, *European Journal of International Relations*, 3(2), pp. 193–237.

Makarychev, A. S. (2009) A Rússia, a Europa e o legado de 1989: conflitos de interpretação, *Relações Internacionais*, September 2009, no. 23, pp. 53–74.

Massari, M. (2007) Russia and the EU ten years on: A relationship in search of definition, *The International Spectator: Italian Journal of International Affairs*, 42(1), pp. 1–15.

Marsh, S. (2008) EU–Russia security relations and the survey of Russian Federation foreign policy: One year on, *European Security*, 17(2/3), pp. 185–208.

Nitoiu, C. (2011) Reconceptualizing 'cooperation' in EU–Russia relations, *Perspectives on European Politics and Society*, 12(4), pp. 426–476.

Popescu, N. & Wilson, A. (2009) *The Limits of Enlargement-lite: European and Russian power in the troubled neighbourhood* (London: European Council on Foreign Relations).

Potemkina, O. (2010) EU–Russia cooperation on the common space of freedom, security and justice – a challenge or an opportunity?, *European Security*, 19(4), 551–568.

Radchuk, T. (2011) Contested neighbourhood, or how to reconcile the differences, *Journal of Communist Studies and Transition Politics*, 27(1), pp. 22–49.

Radio Free Europe/Radio Liberty (2009) At EU–Russia summit, signs of strategic division, not strategic partnership', RFE/RL [online], 22 May. Available at http://www.rferl.org/content/At_EURussia_Summit_Signs_Of_Strategic_Division_Not_Strategic_Partnership/1737474.html (accessed 1 June 2012).

Ria Novosti (2009) EU's Eastern Partnership program not against Moscow – Lavrov, *Ria Novosti* [online], 28 April. Available at http://en.rian.ru/russia/20090428/121350475.html (accessed 1 June 2012).

Road Map on the Common Economic Space (2005) Available at http://www.russianmission.eu/userfiles/file/road_map_on_the_common_economic_space_2005_english.pdf (accessed 1 June 2012).

Sakwa, R. (2011) Russia's identity: Between the 'domestic' and the 'international', *Europe–Asia Studies*, 63(6), pp. 957–975.

Simmerl, G. (2011) A critical constructivist perspective on global multi-level governance. Discursive struggles among multiple actors in a globalized political space. Unpublished manuscript, Berlin, Freie Universität Berlin. Available at http://www.academia.edu/499659/A_Critical_Constructivist_Perspective_on_Global_Multi-Level_Governance (accessed 6 December 2012).

The Foreign Policy Concept of the Russian Federation (2008) Available at http://archive.kremlin.ru/eng/text/docs/2008/07/204750.shtml (accessed 1 June 2012).

Tolstrup, J. (2009) Studying a negative external actor: Russia's management of stability and instability in the 'Near Abroad', *Democratization*, 16(5), pp. 922–944.

Trenin, D. (2009) Russia's spheres of interests, not influence, *The Washington Quarterly*, 32(4), pp. 3–22.

Tsygankov, A. P. (2006) *Russia's Foreign Policy: Change and continuity in national identity* (Maryland: Rowman & Littlefield Publishers).

Tumanov, S., Gasparishvili, A. & Romanova, E. (2011) Russia–EU relations, or how the Russians really view the EU, *Journal of Communist Studies and Transition Politics*, 27(1), pp. 120–141.

Zehfuss, M. (2001) Constructivisms in international relations: Wendt, Onuf and Kratochwil, in: K. M. Fierke & K. E. Jørgensen (Eds) *Constructing International Relations: The next generation*, pp. 54–75 (New York: M. E. Sharpe).

Zehfuss, M. (2006) Constructivism and identity: A dangerous liaison, in: S. Guzzini & A. Leander (Eds) *Constructivism and international relations: Alexander Wendt and his critics*, pp. 93–117 (London: Routledge).

Index

absolute advantage 32
acquis communautaire 46, 96
Adler-Nissen, Rebecca 40–2, 43–4, 45, 49, 53
adversarial disposition 49
anti-dumping laws 21–38
anti-subsidy measures 26
apathy 16
Arif, Kader 29
Ashton, Catherine 63, 64, 79–80, 82, 83, 86, 88, 89

background ideational ability 70–1
Barroso, José Manuel 27, 79, 82, 86, 88
Bickerton, Chris 77
Blinkevičiūtė, Vilija 32
Bourdieu, Pierre 40, 42–6, 50
'Brussels bubble' 4, 39–58; *see also* European Parliament
bureaucratic politics 65

Carlsnaes, Walter 65
Caspary, Daniel 29, 33
Castex, Françoise 31
chains of equivalence 23, 24, 29, 30, 32, 33
China 29, 32
citizenship 10, 17
Civilian Planning and Conduct Capability (CPCC) 64
climate change 86–7
co-operation 51, 52, 55
cognitive approach to FP analysis 65, 70–1
Cold War 24, 28, 95, 97, 102
Collective Security Treaty Organisation 98
Committee for Civilian Aspects of Crisis Management (CIVCOM) 64
Committee of Permanent Representatives (COREPER) 64
Common Economic Space 101
Common Foreign and Security Policy (CFSP) 59, 61
Common Security and Defence Policy (CSDP) 59, 61
common sense 15

Common Strategy on Russia 100
communication 2, 3, 13, 16, 23, 47, 70, 78
communicative discourse 78
Community of Independent States 98
competition: distortion of 29–30; Russian shared neighbourhood 99–100
Conference of Presidents 47, 51
consensus 47, 48, 72; anti-dumping laws 23; culture of 47, 49, 54, 55; unfair trade 28, 34
constructivism: critical 6, 94–5, 104; social 19, 66, 68–70; structural 43
coordinative discourse 63–5, 73, 78
Copenhagen Conference 86, 87
Cox, Robert 79
critical constructivism 6, 94–5, 104
critical discourse analysis 5
cultural spill-over 10–11

De Gucht, Karel 22, 30, 32, 33
de Sarnez, Marielle 29, 32, 33
De Veyrac, Christine 28–9, 32
Delanty, Gerald 78
democratization 81–2
development policy 86
disaffection 16
discourse 1–2, 6, 23–5, 67, 77–9; communicative 78; coordinative 63–5, 73, 78; critical analysis 5
discursive institutionalism 66, 67, 69
disposition 39, 45, 51, 52, 55; adversarial 49
diversity 79, 81
doxa 45–6, 53–5

Eastern Neighbourhood 6, 92–107
Eastern Partnership initiative 96
empty signifiers 14
environmental dumping 33–4
ethnography 39–58
EU *see* European Union
Euro zone crisis 6
European Commission 3, 22
European Convention (2001–2003) 62–3
European Defense Agency (EDA) 65

INDEX

European External Action Service (EEAS) 63, 64
European identity 2, 8–20
European integration theory 2, 3–4, 9, 10–11; alternative paradigms 12–13; complementary paradigms 13–15; paradigmatic nature 11–12; political myth 4, 9, 15–18
European Neighbourhood Policy (EPN) 3, 82–4, 95–6, 103–4
European Parliament (EP) 3, 4–5, 23; co-ordinators 51; Conference of Presidents 47, 51; consensus culture 54; formal offices 50; perceived preference coherence 52; plenary roll call votes 40; position on unfair trade 25–8; sociological analysis 42–6; as transnational political field 46–55
European Security Strategy (ESS) 84–6, 96
European studies 17–18
European Union (EU): Institute for Security Studies (ISS) 65; Military Committee (EUMC) 64; Military Staff (EUMS) 64; as promoter of peace 79–81; relations with Russia 100–4; Satellite Centre (EUSC) 65
external relations 10, 76–91; European Neighbourhood Policy (EPN) 3, 82–4, 95–6, 103; and foreign policy 62–3; global well-being 86–7; good neighbourliness 6, 82–4; with Russia *see* Russian shared neighbourhood; security 84–6

fair trade 26
fairness 21
Farage, Nigel 49
Fernandes, José Manuel 32
Ferrero-Waldner, Benita 102, 104
Fidanza, Carlo 30
field 43–4, 46–8
floating signifiers 4, 21, 23–5, 28, 34; unfair trade as 28–34
Fontana, Lorenzo 31
foreground discursive abilities 70, 71
foreign policy 5–6, 59–75; coordinative discourse 63–5, 73; European vs. EU 61–2; and external relations 62–3; *see also* external relations
foreign policy analysis 65–72; bureaucratic politics approach 67–8; cognitive approach 65, 70–1; discursive approach 66, 67, 69; material reality 67–8; organizational process approach 65, 71–2; psychological approach 67–8; social constructivist approach 66, 68–70; theoretical framework 66–7
FP *see* foreign policy

global well-being 86–7

good neighbourliness 5, 6, 82–4; *see also* external relations
Great Depression 31
group dynamics 71–2

habitus 45, 48–9
Hobsbawm, Eric 13
'how-possible' questions 14

ideology 4, 8, 15
inclusiveness 81
individualism 15
institutionalism 41; discursive 66, 67, 69; neoliberal 65; new 67
intergovernmentalism 3, 10, 18
international relations *see* external relations
International Trade Committee (INTR) 25

Kalinoski, Jarosław 31
Kamiński, Michał Tomasz 26
Köstinger, Elisabeth 30, 31, 32
Kuhn, Thomas 9, 11
Kyoto Treaty 87

La Via, Giovanni 30
language game 11–12, 19
Latin America 31–2
Lavrov, Sergei 102
linguistics 11, 13
Løkkegaard, Morten 33

market 84
Martin, Hans-Peter 29
'meanings-in-use' 14
Melo, Nuno 30
MEPs *see* European Parliament; and individual MEPs
Mitrany, David 10
mobility 84
money 84
Monnet, Jean 10
Moreira, Vital 27
multi-level governance 2–3
multilateralism 86–7
Muscardini, Cristiana 32

narratives 77–9; democratization 81–2; security 84–6
nation states 12, 76–7
nationalism 12
neo-functionalism 3, 8, 10, 18
neo-realist approach to FP analysis 65
neoliberal institutionalism 65
new institutionalism 67
nodal points 24–5
non-market economies, trade with 28–30

INDEX

ontological support 78
organizational process approach to FP analysis 65, 71–2

participation 81
Partnership for Modernisation 101
path dependency 79
Patrão Neves, Maria do Céu 27
Patten, Chris 63, 81
peace, promotion of 79–81
Pirillo, Mario 27
political capital 44, 49–53
political commitment 82
political myth 4, 9, 15–18
Political and Security Committee (PSC) 64
Politico-Military Group 64
polity 2, 3
post-structuralism 3
Prague Eastern Partnership Summit 97
praxis 94
predatory pricing 22
preference formation 71
process and production methods 31
protectionism 27, 29
Provera, Fiorello 30
psychological approach to FP analysis 65
Putin, Vladimir 85, 98

quasi-individualism 12, 13, 15, 17

rationalism 16, 17
realist approach to FP analysis 65
reciprocity 28, 29, 32, 33
regime of truth 24, 25
rhetorical entrapment 78, 79
Rinaldi, Niccolò 27
role theory 66
Rossi, Oreste 31
Rumford, Chris 78
Russian shared neighbourhood 92–107; competition for 99–100; critical constructivism 94–5, 104; EU perspective 95–7; Russian perspective 97–9; security 94–5
Russian-EU relations 100–4
Ryner, Magnus 19

Saïfi, Tokia 27
Schlyter, Carl 33
Schmidt, Vivien 67, 69, 70–1, 73, 78
scientific paradigm 9, 11
security 84–6; European Security Strategy (ESS) 84–6, 96; Russian shared neighbourhood 94–7
self-reflexiveness 8–9
Servent, Ripoll 53–4

signifiers: empty 14; floating *see* floating signifiers; nodal points 24–5
Silvestris, Sergio Paulo Francesco 30
Single Economic Space 98
Smith, Hazel 62
Smith, Michael 62
social construction 19
social constructivism 19; FP analysis 66, 68–70
social dumping 30–4
socio-cognitive approach to FP 67, 70
sociological analysis (Bourdieu) 42–6; doxa 45–6, 53–5; field 43–4, 46–8; habitus 45, 48–9; political capital 44, 49–53; strategies 44–5, 49–53; structural constructivism 43
Solana, Javier 87, 89
solidarity 85
stigma management 43
storylines 23–5
strategy 44–5, 49–53
structural constructivism 43
Sturdy, Robert 27
supranational institutions 12

Trade Defence Instruments 4, 21–38
trade liberalisation 26, 33
trade with non-market economies 28–30
trade protection 21–38
trade remedies 22; anti-dumping laws 22
transactionalism 12–13
Treaty of Lisbon 23, 26, 64

unfair trade 4, 21–38; as distortion of competition 29–30; as environmental dumping 33–4; European Parliament position 25–8; as floating signifier 28–34; as social dumping 30–3; trade with non-market economies 28–30
Union for Foreign Affairs and Security Policy 64
USA 34; Hawley-Smoot Tariff Act 31

van Dijk, Teun 67, 70, 71
Van Rompuy, Herman 49
Viner, Jacob 22

Waever, Ole 69
Weber, Henri 29
White, Brian 66
Włosowicz, Jacek 27
World Trade Organization (WTO) 22; Singapore issues 30

Zahradil, Jan 27
Zampeti, Beviglia 31